To My
Darling
who defines the 21st C.
in the 21st

XX

Hilary

Christmas 2008

Van Day Truex

Van Day Truex

The Man Who Defined Twentieth-Century Taste and Style

ADAM LEWIS

Foreword by Albert Hadley

Viking Studio

VIKING STUDIO
Published by the Penguin Group
Penguin Putnam Inc., 375 Hudson Street,
New York, New York 10014, U.S.A.
Penguin Books Ltd, 27 Wrights Lane,
London W8 5TZ, England
Penguin Books Australia Ltd, Ringwood,
Victoria, Australia
Penguin Books Canada Ltd, 10 Alcorn Avenue,
Toronto, Ontario, Canada M4V 3B2
Penguin Books (N.Z.) Ltd, 182-190 Wairau Road,
Auckland 10, New Zealand

Penguin Books Ltd, Registered Offices:
Harmondsworth, Middlesex, England

First published in 2001 by Viking Studio,
a member of Penguin Putnam Inc.

10 9 8 7 6 5 4 3 2 1

The endpapers are a photograph of the carpet "Terra" designed by Van Day Truex. Courtesy of Edward Fields, Inc.,
New York.

LIBRARY OF CONGRESS CATALOGING-IN-PUBLICATION DATA
Lewis, Adam
   Van Day Truex, the man who defined twentieth-
century taste and style / Adam Lewis.
      p. cm.
   Includes index.
   ISBN 0-670-03024-4
   1. Truex, Van Day, d. 1979. 2. Interior decorators—
United States—Biography. 3. Parsons School of Design. 4.
Tiffany and Company. I. Title: Van Day Truex. II. Title.

   NK2004.3.T78 L49 2001
   745.4'492—dc21   00-054997

Printed in England by Butler & Tanner Ltd.
Set in Bembo
Designed by Jaye Zimet

PHOTO CREDITS

John T. Hill: xiv, xviii, 192, 209, 221, 222, 223, 224.
Ruth N. Jacobson, xii, photograph by Jesse Gerstein.
William P. Steele: 236, 240, 241, 242, 243.
Josiah Wedgewood & Sons Limited: 196.
Parsons School of Design: 25, 31, The Anna-Maria and
   Stephen Kellen Archives of Parsons School of De-
   sign.
Tiffany and Company: 189, 200, 202, © 1960, Tiffany and
   Company; 201, © Tiffany and Company, photog-
   rapher Erik Kvasvik, *Tiffany's 150 Years* by John Lor-
   ing published by Doubleday & Company, Inc.; 206,
   © Tiffany and Company, photographer Jesse Ger-
   stein, *Tiffany's 150 Years* by John Loring published by
   Doubleday & Company, Inc.
Vogue: 80, 118, photographs by Roger Schall. By permis-
   sion of Condé Nast.
House & Garden: 160 (top), 161, photographs by Andre
   Kertész; 225, 226, 239, photographs by Horst; 160
   (bottom), photograph by Haanel Cassidy. By permission of Condé Nast.
Adam Lewis: 214, 246.
Van Day Truex: xxiv, 47, 48, 49, 56, 57, 61, 62, 64, 66, 74,
   85, 86, 89, 90, 102, 103, 104, 106, 112, 113, 121, 123,
   128, 136, 146, 149, 155, 184, 216, 217, 219, 230.
Van Day Truex photography albums and scrapbooks: ii, 3,
   4, 10, 14, 17, 18, 22, 54, 59, 70, 77, 92, 99, 105, 116,
   130, 150, 152, 157, 164, 180, 183, 199, 205, 208, 214,
   232.

To

Molly and Thom

for reasons they know best

Foreword

*A*dam Lewis has produced a highly significant, provocative, and embracing book that chronicles the life and times of a man whose contribution to the design world in the twentieth century was paramount.

Van Day Truex: educator, designer, artist, and friend. In this book one is transported on the journey of his life, from his early childhood in Kansas, through his student days at the New York School of Fine and Applied Arts and his roles as director of the school's Paris branch on the place des Vosges, to head of the New York School and finally his time as the design director for Tiffany & Co.

The early decades of the last century—the time between the two great wars, the telling years—were the formative period of Truex's creative and social life. In Paris he was a key player, a participant in the creative forces that encompassed all art forms: music, dance, painting, and sculpture, as well as literature, architecture, fashion, and the decorative arts. In the great City of Light, his design philosophy was crystallized into a personal, extremely selective format that would serve him and the future design community with outstanding clarity.

Lewis's account of Truex's return to New York at the outbreak of World War II to become the president of the school—soon to be known as the Parsons School of Design, having been renamed for its late founder, Frank

Alvah Parsons—is well documented and told with candor and compassion.

We are made aware, here, of the enormous influence that Truex and his design philosophy had on vast numbers of students who were guided by his knowledge and sophisticated taste to produce works of outstanding quality in the realm of contemporary American design. We are also led to see that Truex's philosophy of design and the decorative arts was based strongly on classical principles, while at the same time he was influenced by the dramatic mode of the *grand-siècle,* the golden age of France. It is clear, too, that his credo of design encompassed the arts that emerged in Europe during the first quarter of the twentieth century.

The book carries us forward to experience firsthand Truex's role as the arbiter of taste for some of America's most prominent companies, organizations that are themselves recognized as great innovators of design. All along the way, the reader is brought into close proximity to the man himself. In revealing Truex's human qualities, Lewis gives us a unique chance to respond with our own meaningful feelings.

Presenting a clear view of the recent history of interior design and the people who shaped it, Lewis's book will be a valuable tool and reference for anyone interested in interior design and the decorative arts. He is to be highly commended on a work that focuses on the dedication and caring of the individual who set the standard for taste and style in our century, a man whose voice was heard with clarity at home and abroad. Expounding on Van Day Truex's strongly held opinions, Adam Lewis affords us the opportunity to perceive this man's passion to establish design, when viewed from the highest level of appropriateness, not as an abstract exercise but as art, accurately reflecting all aspects of civilized life.

Albert Hadley, New York, 2001

Acknowledgments

*I*n order to express my gratitude to the individuals and institutions that helped with this book, and to share with my readers their importance, I have listed them in specific categories. Should there be any omissions, I offer my apologies.

In reading other writers' acknowledgments, I find that more often than not, authors mention their editor last. For me, Ray Roberts, my editor, is primary. From the first time we met to discuss the Truex biography until the complete manuscript was delivered to him, he gave me immeasurable guidance. His remarkable expertise in the craft of writing, his unerring taste, his love of the English language, and, finally, his humor—that gift so necessary to relieve the solitude of writing—are without equal.

Before I list the categories of people who helped with this book, there are eight individuals who must be singled out for their unique contributions. In the early stages of my writing, the late John Pierrepont and his wife Nancy welcomed me into their home and made available to me Truex's personal papers and scrapbooks. Without them and their generous spirit, my interest in Truex would have never gone beyond my initial curiosity. Albert Hadley— Truex's student, a member of his faculty, and his trusted friend—provided history and comments, from his own experience, that have been infallible. John Hill, my former teacher and a photographer and designer, gave me help and professional advice that I can never repay. John, along with Ray Roberts, kept ever before me the challenge of producing a responsible document. Susanna Barrows, the niece of Stanley Barrows, a former member of the Parsons faculty, made available all of her uncle's records, class notes, and correspondence, as well as his oral history of Parsons. Joseph Braswell, a Truex student, supplied firsthand knowledge of the life at Parsons School of Design during the post–World War II period and a wealth of information on the past fifty years of interior design in New York City. Claudia and John Thomas, spirited friends of innate taste, were the first, when reviewing my initial research, to say, "You've got a book on your hands. Write it."

The most important group of people to provide information on Truex's background were members of his family. While no members of his immediate family survive, documents and photographs were provided by his Day and Van Landingham relatives. I offer my gratitude to Diane Day Sherman, William J. Pease, Richard E. Brock, Ruth Brock, Thomas B. Brock, and Shelly Galloway.

Staff at the Parsons School of Design, past and present—especially Ted Barber, archivist; Tim Gunn, head of the fashion department; and David Levy, former Parsons president and current chairman of the Corcoran Gallery of Art in Washington—were cooperative and untiring in their efforts to provide accurate information. The other institutions whose staff gave assistance are the Cooper-Hewitt National Design Museum, New York City; the Smithsonian Archives of American Art, Washington, D.C.; the Musée de la Légion d'Honneur, Paris; Evergreen House, Baltimore, Maryland; the Filson Club, Lexington, Kentucky; University of Wisconsin, Oshkosh; the public schools of Saint Anthony, Idaho, Concordia, Kansas, and Rice Lake, Wisconsin; the J. C. Penney Archives, Dallas, Texas; and the New York Public Library, the New York Society Library, the Guggenheim Museum, the Museum of Modern Art, and the Metropolitan Museum of Art, all in New York.

Most certainly this book would not have been possible without the assistance of Tiffany & Company. To the following people who were or are now a part of Tiffany's, I extend my gratitude: John Loring, Pierce MacGuire, Elizabeth Franceschini, Linda Buckley, Farnham Lefferts, Ronald Schwarz, Michel Barcun, David Hall, Annamarie Sandecki, Mary Ann Aurora, and George O'Brien.

The many friends and associates of Truex's who provided factual and anecdotal material for his biography include Laurance and Isabel Roberts, Cynthia Sainsbury and her late husband, Barry, Walter Lees, Burnet Pavitt, Brooke Astor, Rosamond Bernier, Joe Downing, Jane Eakin, Melvin Dwork, Jay Hyde Crawford, Murray Douglas, Paige Rense, Kenneth Paul Block, Daniel Kiener, Bernard Devaux, Letitia Baldridge, Donald Brooks, Amber Lightfoot-Walker, Carrie Donovan, Ethel Smith, Betty Sherrill, Harry Hinson, Richard Jenrette, John Richardson, Bowden Broadwater, Louis Auchincloss, Florence Knoll Bassett, Ashton Hawkins, Sarah Tomerlin Lee, Eleanor Lambert, Tony Marshall, Geoffery Gates, Jr., Bunny Williams, Alan Campbell, Ann Thorn, Charles Sevigny, Yves Vidal, Helene de Breteuil, Lewis Lapham, Marguerite Littman, Deeda Blair, James Davison, Jacqueline Tahon, Michael Mahoney, Paul Peralta-Ramos, Arturo Peralta-Ramos, Patricia Cavendish O'Neil, Harry Cipriani, Fabio Pizzoni, Philip Johnson, ZoZo de Ravenel, Harry Hinson, and Hubert de Givenchy.

Among the many people to whom I am grateful for assistance are Karen Yaeger, Solange Herter, Eileen Finletter, Eleanor Dwight, Larry Hughes, Harriett Mays, François de Bené, Willoughby Newton, François and Cecile Nourissier, Nicholas and Dorothy Krul, John Landau, Keith and Eileen Dawson, Liza Hyde, Michael Stier, Charles Scheips, Jr., Stan Friedman, Ernest Rosenberg, Ann Brockschmidt, Joan Gers, and Anne Cox Chambers. Finally, I am grateful to my agent, Deborah Geltman, and Jaye Zimet, who designed my book.

Contents

Introduction

$\mathcal{D}$elineating "today's outstanding decorators" in the *New York Times Book of Interior Design and Decoration,* published in 1976, Norma Skurka begins with Van Day Truex and bestows on him the title "arbiter of American taste." Writing in *House and Garden* in 1986, Mark Hampton distinguishes Truex as "the legendary decorator." Later, in his *Mark Hampton on Decorating,* 1989, he would extol Truex's "prophetic sense of style" and define him as "a man of enormous influence" and "one of the most influential teachers of design of this century."

One evening early in the summer of 1995, soon after I moved to New York City, John and Dorothy Hill, friends from Connecticut, visited my new apartment. As I prepared dinner, the Hills looked through my collection of books on architecture and interior design. Later, as we were having our meal, either John or Dorothy (I can't remember which) expressed surprise that I did not have Van Day Truex's book on interior decorating. While I knew who Truex was, I confessed that I was unaware of his having written such a book. They were both relatively sure he had, and they proceeded to share with me the story of a trip they had taken to Provence in late June 1969. John had been assigned to photograph Truex's house Chaumet, outside the village of Gargas, near Apt, for a feature story in the *New York Times Magazine;* for the same article, "The Best of Two Worlds," by Barbara Plumb, he had also pho-

The first piece of sculpture that Truex bought in Paris in 1925, the working cast of a bust commissioned by Queen Victoria, and the last piece of sculpture he bought in 1979, Naexa-Alkyad *by Douglas Abdel. The photograph was taken at the New York apartment of Albert Hadley in 1984.*

tographed Truex's Park Avenue apartment in New York. At the time, Truex held a unique position as consultant for design at Tiffany & Co.

Both John and Dorothy vividly remembered Truex's refined taste and innate sense of style, evident in Chaumet's every detail. Most impressive, they thought, was the way he had managed to maintain, in a modern renovation, the inherent simplicity of a rustic eighteenth-century farmhouse. They remarked on his use of unadorned native stone in the basic construction and unglazed terra cotta tiles for all the floors, and described his decorating choices: the simple bamboo furniture made in a neighboring town; the lamps converted from old wine bottles, adorned with paper shades; the modest cotton and linen fabrics; and the monochromatic color scheme—all beige—for both upstairs and downstairs.

They recalled that there were very few decorative accessories in the

A view of Truex's New York apartment, 1969.

house. They remembered seeing some trompe l'oeil plates on the dining-room walls, from the collection Truex had designed for Tiffany's, and a few pieces of primitive African art and some ancient French farm implements in the living room, but that was all. Dorothy was especially intrigued by the natural landscape of the property around the house and the abundance of wild yellow broom and red poppies, which Truex allowed to grow untended in the meadow below the terrace where they had their midday meal.

As they talked about the lunch Truex served, John said he would always remember it as one of the simplest, most beautifully presented, and most delicious meals he had ever eaten. He elaborated, "The medallions of veal were perfectly cooked, seasoned with only a little salt and pepper, *herbes de Provence,* and fresh lemon. The salad and cheese tray that followed was so exquisitely arranged that it could have been readily photographed for a promotion of the local cuisine. The Cavaillon melon for dessert was perfectly ripe, and Truex's presentation with fresh cherries was worthy of a feature spread in *Gourmet* magazine."

Dorothy had other memories of Truex, from an earlier time, when she worked at Tiffany's after her graduation from Smith College. She spoke of the original silver and china patterns he had designed and talked at length about the esteem in which he had been held: "He was revered. Members of the Tiffany's staff were always respectfully aware when Mr. Truex entered their department."

In addition to working as a photographer, John was a member of the faculty at the Yale School of Art and Architecture. From his perspective as a teacher, he talked about Truex's reputation as an innovative educator during his years as president of the Parsons School of Design. He added that many of the people associated with Parsons during Truex's tenure, either as critics or as advisers—including Alexey Brodovitch, Paul Rand, Bradbury Thompson, and Philip Johnson—had at one time or another held similar positions at Yale.

Prompted by the Hills' enthusiasm about Truex, I stopped in the following day at Archivia, a shop specializing in books on interior design and architecture, to inquire about the volume they thought he had written. While the saleswoman, Ann Brockschmidt, said that Archivia did not have the book, she did verify that a work entitled *Interiors, Character and Color,* by Van Day Truex, had indeed been published in 1980. (I would later discover that this was a year after Truex's death.) I left the shop feeling confident that I would find the book in the library of the Parsons School of Design.

Several days later, at Parsons's Gimbel Library, I was told by the young man at the circulation desk that the library did not have the book I was looking for, and that moreover, quite to my surprise, he had never heard of its author. After I saw him write "Van de Truex" on a notepad, I gave him the correct spelling and explained that Truex had been president of Parsons for ten years. Obviously embarrassed, the young man excused himself to ask the research librarian, Jenny Tobias, for assistance. When informed of my request, Tobias admitted that she had never heard of Truex, either, and confirmed that Gimbel did not have a copy of his book. Genuinely eager to help me, she accessed her interlibrary computer reference to see if the book was available anywhere else in New York City. Her search turned up a single copy at the Cooper-Hewitt National Design Museum, on East Ninety-first Street.

The following day, at Cooper-Hewitt, I finally got to see *Interiors, Character and Color.* To my disappointment, it was not really a book at all but a pamphlet. It contained little text and resembled the type of promotional brochure frequently distributed without charge to interior decorators by furniture and fabric manufacturers. Later research would reveal that the pamphlet had been a "dividend" appended to a large-format book entitled *Color,* published by Knapp Press, the original publisher of the magazine *Architectural Digest.* The brief text was a compilation of excerpts taken from a series of articles, "Van Day Truex on Design," that Truex had written for *Architectural*

Digest in 1977 and 1978. Considering the modest nature of *Interiors, Character and Color,* I was surprised that it was included in the rare-books collection of the National Design Museum.

Seeing Truex's book and knowing that he had been president of Parsons and design director for Tiffany's stimulated my desire to learn more about him. I found it curious that he was now so little known, even at the school of which he had been president, when as recently as 1969 he had been prominent enough to merit a feature article in the *New York Times Magazine* on his decorating talents. (Much later, I would discover that the 1969 article for which John Hill had taken the photographs was but one of many such pieces that the *Times* had run on Truex.) I reasoned that if the Parsons School of Design had no information on him, the two most logical places for me to look next were the New York Public Library and Tiffany & Co.

The following week, my friend Thomas Chu and I researched the files of the public library and found most of the articles that Truex had written for *Architectural Digest* in the late 1970s. At the end of each of them, Truex was identified by the editors as "one of the most respected names in interior design." The library files also produced articles published about Truex between 1939 and 1979. Included among these references were laudatory reviews of exhibitions of his paintings, mounted at some of New York's most prestigious galleries in the 1930s, 1940s, and 1950s. His name frequently appeared, too, in articles about interior decoration, and in the March 1939 issue of *Vogue,* he was described as the most famous American living in Paris. Here again, I had to ask, If Truex had been such an important figure from 1939 to 1979, why had he seemingly disappeared, in less than twenty years, from the vanguard of interior decoration and design?

Soon after completing my research at the public library, I met with John Loring, the present design director at Tiffany's. Like John and Dorothy Hill, Loring had many Truex stories, and he was filled with admiration for the man who had hired him in 1978 as his successor. Loring had no specific information on Truex's background, but he said he thought he was originally from Wyoming. Before I left Tiffany's, Loring made the necessary arrangements for me to visit the company archives in Parsippany, New Jersey.

A view of Truex's dining area in 1969. The French chairs were a gift from William Odom.

When I got to Parsippany, I was disappointed to find no personal information on Truex in the archives. There was one large file containing his original sketches for President and Mrs. Lyndon Johnson's White House china, but no further documentation of the project seemed to exist. Annamarie Sandecki, the archivist, explained that maintaining an archive was a relatively new endeavor for Tiffany's. Essentially, their records gave no information on Truex that I did not already have from reading *The Tiffany Touch,* Joseph Purtell's history of the company.

In early September 1995, I received a telephone call from Ted Barber, who had recently been appointed the archivist at Parsons. Barber had heard about my visit to the school from the librarians, and he offered to share with me what little information he had about Truex. With his assistance, I went through numerous boxes of unorganized materials. Parsons, like Tiffany's, had just begun organizing its archives, and almost nothing of any significance to my research surfaced. I did establish that Truex had graduated from Parsons (then known as the New York School of Fine and Applied Arts) in 1926 and immediately thereafter been made a member of the faculty. The school catalogs also confirmed that he had been president from 1942 until 1952. A cryptic paragraph in David Levy's "History of Parsons," a doctoral degree thesis submitted to New York University in 1979, implied that Truex's tenure had ended under somewhat ominous circumstances. If this was true, yet another compelling question presented itself: how did he go from a debacle at Parsons to the prestigious position of design director at Tiffany & Co.? I was beginning to think about writing a biography of this elusive man. I was convinced that Truex was important enough to justify a record of his life and accomplishments.

As my research progressed, I remembered that soon after the death of Jacqueline Kennedy Onassis, in May 1994, the local evening news had shown hordes of curiosity seekers lined up at City Hall to read her will. In the course of the broadcast, the reporter had explained that the will of any person who dies in New York City is open to the public. Knowing that Truex had died in New York on April 24, 1979, I realized that I had a new avenue for research. The following day, in the municipal Office of Probate, I was allowed to see Truex's will, a copy of his death certificate, and an inventory of the apartment in which he had died. From these papers, I learned that a John Pierrepont had been the executor of Truex's estate. While the Metropolitan Museum of Art was named as his chief beneficiary, receiving nearly five hundred thousand dollars, three people—John Pierrepont, William Baldwin, and Walter Lees—had also received bequests. According to the Consumer Price Index, in the year 1995, the bequest to the Metropolitan Museum would have amounted to slightly over a million dollars.

That night, I called the only John Pierrepont listed in the New York City telephone directory and explained to the voice on the other end of the line that I was doing research for a book about a man named Van Day Truex. Pierrepont's immediate response was, "It's about time somebody did this. Come over to my apartment tomorrow, and I'll do all I can to help you."

Both John Pierrepont and his wife, Nancy, an established interior decorator, had many stories to tell about Truex. Neither of them could say enough about his decorating talents, his original designs, his paintings, and his refined taste. Pierrepont had been both Truex's financial adviser and the executor of his estate, but when I asked him a few questions about Truex's personal life and background, he said, "I knew him for nearly twenty years and I never heard him, even once, mention his family." After settling Truex's estate, Pierrepont had stored his few remaining personal effects in his office. Included among these things were nine large photo albums organized by Truex and dating from 1923 to 1975. They contained pictures of him with some of the most prominent figures in fashion, interior design, and international society. John Pierrepont knew many of the people in the photographs and offered to introduce me to those who were still living. Through the entrée he provided, I began interviewing people in New York City. Everyone I met supplied leads, and frequently introductions, to others who had known Truex. The interviews and my research would ultimately lead me to the Midwest, California, England, France, and Italy.

Without exception, all of the individuals I spoke with said that Truex had always blithely responded to inquiries about his past with statements such as "I was born during a cyclone on the western plains of Kansas" or "I came from way out west in Wyoming." The question is, why did he so studiously avoid revealing anything about his past? One of the most consistent memories that my sources had of Truex concerned the elegance and refined style of his wardrobe and his innate flair for wearing clothes. Men and women alike mentioned the powerful impact he always made entering a room.

The people and places in the photographs in Truex's scrapbooks are not always identified, and the dates, if given at all, are often conflicting. The dates that *do* appear, however, confirm that he studied in New York City from the fall of 1923 through the spring of 1925, finished his course in Paris in 1926, and taught at the Paris branch of the school from 1927 until 1939. We know that the span of Truex's life, from 1904 to 1979, was marked by dramatic social, political, and economic changes worldwide. His scrapbook photographs show him with many of those who brought about these changes. In the pictures, he appears over and over not as a spectator, but in close company with some of the richest, the most famous, and the most talented people in the world.

As my research progressed, it became obvious to me that Truex had arrived in New York in 1923 and invented himself. He made himself, a poor boy from Kansas, into the most socially prominent educator and designer of his day. Through hard work and rigid discipline, he earned distinction in two careers. His first success came at Parsons, where he rose to become president of the institution, and his second at Tiffany's, where he was director of design.

To understand the importance of Truex's contributions at Parsons and his influence on interior design, it is necessary to remember that before the turn of the century, such work was directed by architects and upholsterers. Two significant events changed all that and led to the abandonment of the Victorian approach to home furnishings. First, in 1897, Edith Wharton and Ogden Codman, Jr., published *The Decoration of Houses,* the first book on the subject of interior decoration. And second, in 1904, Elsie de Wolfe received a contract to decorate the Colony Club, a women's club then located on Madison Avenue in New York City. Together, these two occurrences gave rise to interior design as we know it today.

At the Parsons School of Design, Truex was at the center of this new profession. He became the head of Parsons when it was still little more than a finishing school for proper young ladies. In Paris during the 1930s and in New York City from 1940 through 1952, Truex was the educator responsible for shaping the minds and talents of the great numbers of young people who entered this new field. Although other influential design philosophies were being forged at the same time, under his leadership, Parsons became the foremost school for interior design. When I interviewed Albert Hadley, America's preeminent interior designer, himself a graduate of Parsons and later a member of the faculty, he firmly maintained, "No one influenced American interior design more than Van Day Truex." The title of an article published in *Connoisseur* magazine in 1979 proclaimed him "The Late Dean of Twentieth-Century Design."

After his years at Parsons, Truex became the design director for Tiffany & Co. In the years he was there, the store evolved into an even more prestigious institution than it had previously been and gained a reputation for unprecedented elegance. John Thomas, the former director of Wedgwood (USA), who worked closely with Truex at Tiffany's, says, "With no discredit to Walter Hoving's merchandising genius, it was Truex who turned Tiffany's around. He had the most refined taste of any person I have ever known."

Truex's own writings and interviews with those who knew him make it clear that he loved the art of ancient cultures and classic art, especially the arts of eighteenth-century France; that he was a fierce defender of contemporary art and design; and that he looked expectantly to the arts of the future. He was foremost a perfectionist, intolerant of cheap imitations, and demanded the highest standards of "design judgment" (his definition of taste) from himself and everyone around him. He believed passionately that the forms and colors of nature were the greatest inspiration for design. His philosophy on how to achieve the best was simple: "Control. Distill. Edit."

When Truex was made a Chevalier de la Légion d'Honneur, the citation listing his distinguished accomplishments as an educator, painter, interior decorator, and designer opened with the order's highest praise: "Monsieur Van Day Truex, Le Connaisseur des Arts Décoratifs."

A Weekend in the Country

*A*fter Van Day Truex retired as design director for Tiffany's in 1962, he continued to work as special consultant to the chairman of the company, Walter Hoving. He spent his winters in New York City and each April went to France, where he lived for eight months of the year in the region of Provence known as the Lubéron Valley. There, in the village of Ménerbes, in 1969, he built a house that would become the fulfillment of his lifelong search for simplicity. For him, the Lubéron was the most perfect place on earth.

After eight years in Ménerbes, in 1977, with no warning and for no apparent reason, Truex began having blackout seizures. Often he would find himself lying on the floor of his house without any recollection of falling or any idea of how long he had been there. At first these fainting spells were irregular, but then suddenly they began occurring with greater frequency. When he went for an examination at the regional hospital in nearby Avignon, the doctors diagnosed a serious heart problem. The physicians explained that they were not equipped to treat his condition and recommended that he see a cardiologist at the American Hospital in Neuilly-sur-Seine. The thought of being hospitalized in Paris and the anticipated cost of medical care were extremely unsettling to Truex. As an American citizen, he was not eligible for French government–funded medical care, and he knew that his limited

Chaumet, Gargas, Provence.

health-insurance policy would not cover the costs of surgery, hospitalization, and extensive postoperative care. As he struggled with these realities and with the idea of having to leave Provence, his condition worsened, and the seizures became more regular. In October 1978, he made plans to return to New York City.

By sheer coincidence, when Truex was in the midst of the sale of his house in Ménerbes, Walter Hoving, the chairman of Tiffany's, called to say that George O'Brien, who had been hired to replace Truex as design director in 1967, was leaving the company. In desperate need of help, Hoving asked Truex to return immediately and resume his old job. Hoving's proposal included making him a full-time employee of Tiffany's, with all company benefits, including health insurance. While the offer could not have come at a better time, Truex was honest with Hoving about his heart problem. Upon hearing the ominous news, Hoving, with no hesitation, said that the company would pay for Truex to have a complete evaluation at the Mayo Clinic and would cover all expenses for any necessary treatment.

For Truex, the most difficult part of leaving France was having to sell his house in Ménerbes. One of the joys of owning it had been knowing that his original plans and interior design for it were widely appreciated. Over the years he had lived there, the house had been featured many times in leading home-furnishings magazines.

Having to say good-bye to Rory Cameron was Truex's other emotional burden. Cameron lived just outside of Ménerbes, five minutes away by car, and over the years the two men had developed a ritual of having lunch together every day. Often they met for dinner as well. In Ménerbes, Cameron had provided a French counterpart to Truex's friendship with Billy Baldwin in New York City. Unquestionably, Baldwin and Cameron were his closest friends.

Packing for the move to New York City involved few weighty deci-

Rory Cameron, left, with Truex in Ireland.

sions about what to take back to the United States and what to leave in France. Truex had never been sentimental about material things. Certainly his inexpensive rattan furniture was not worth shipping, and he knew that his wardrobe, which consisted entirely of casual clothes, would be useless in Manhattan. His favorite paintings, most of which were his own, were easily packed and shipped, along with his few pieces of primitive African art. The only thing he truly regretted having to sell was "La Contessa," his beige Mercedes convertible, which had been a gift from his longtime friend Mona Bismarck.

On Truex's first day back at Tiffany's, Hoving informed him that his appointment at the Mayo Clinic was scheduled for the following week. After five days of rigorous tests at the Rochester clinic, the doctors confirmed Truex's worst fears. They reported that nothing could be done about his heart ailment and further added that he could die at any time, though they felt that with proper care and rest he might live for a couple of years. They concluded their prognosis with the strong recommendation that he adopt a less stressful life-style. Having heard this foreboding report, Truex returned from Minnesota with his mind made up that as soon as a new design director could be hired at Tiffany's, he would move to the country.

A few months before Truex's return to New York, Billy Baldwin had moved to Nantucket. While no one could ever replace Baldwin in Truex's life,

Albert Hadley.

his longtime friend Albert Hadley was one person in the city on whom he could rely. Immediately after World War II, Hadley had been one of his star pupils at Parsons, and when he graduated, in 1949, Truex had invited him to join the faculty. The two men had always had immeasurable respect for each other. Over the last twelve years, while Truex had been spending most of his time in France, Hadley had built a notable career in interior decorating. First working with Eleanor Brown at McMillen, Inc., and then in partnership with Mrs. Henry Parish II, at Parish-Hadley, Inc., he had become one of the most respected designers in America.

When Truex began thinking seriously about his new house and

new life in the country, he knew that he definitely wanted to live in a village or a small town. Having to drive to the market or the post office or even to the store for the morning newspaper was not his notion of a comfortable life. He had made that mistake years before, when he bought a farmhouse near Gargas, France. Remembering that experience, Truex had no interest in an isolated setting. He knew, too, that he wanted a house with a living room large enough also to serve as a dining room; he imagined having a refectory-style table that would comfortably seat six for dinner. There should be a small kitchen, a powder room on the first floor, and two bedrooms, each with a bath, on the second floor. He very much wished to recapture the simplicity of his house in Ménerbes. Certainly he wanted nothing grand.

When Truex talked about buying a house in the country, Hadley suggested that he look at properties in Litchfield County. Hadley himself frequently visited this northwest corner of Connecticut and thought it would offer Truex the peace and quiet he needed, as well as the perfect setting for him to paint. Truex was intrigued when Hadley told him that the young interior decorators Bunny Williams and John Saladino each had a house in Litchfield County. In Truex's estimation, these two individuals had a degree of talent that set them apart in the world of interior design.

Bunny Williams was the epitome of everything Truex admired in a young lady. She came from a good Southern family and had every hallmark of gentility. While working on the staff of Parish-Hadley, she had earned Albert Hadley's high praise for her decorating abilities, and the imprimatur of the venerable Mrs. Henry Parish II. In Truex's opinion, Saladino was one of the most original interior decorators in New York. The thought of having him as a neighbor was an added incentive to look for a house in Litchfield County. Before becoming a designer, Saladino had studied painting at the Yale School of Art and Architecture, where he had developed a remarkable eye for color. As far as Truex knew, Saladino was the only decorator in New York with such training. He thought the young man's interiors had the aura of a Renaissance painting. Believing that a college education was a definite advantage for any decorator, Truex was especially impressed that Saladino had gone to Yale.

At seventy-four, Truex still wondered if he should have listened to his parents and completed his college degree before moving to New York. When he was with people like Saladino, he was haunted by his own lack of a liberal-arts education. Although he had been fortunate enough to have the personal tutoring of Frank Alvah Parsons and William Odom in art history and period design, Truex always felt he lacked the intellectual acumen that came from formal studies in literature and the humanities. Being fluent in French and having a vast knowledge of eighteenth-century French decorative arts filled in some of the gaps in his education, but not all.

The house hunting began in earnest in April 1979. Since Truex did not own a car, Alan Campbell, a young textile designer who had visited him in France, agreed to drive him up to Connecticut for the weekend. When the two men arrived at the inn in the village near Bunny Williams's house, where they had reserved rooms, the promise of a perfect weekend quickly faded. As Campbell drove into the parking lot, they were met by a crowd of revelers. Well plied with drink, the group was obviously ready for a celebration. The minute Truex and Campbell stepped through the entrance of the inn, they were overcome by the smell of beer and cigar smoke wafting from the adjoining tavern. As they spoke with the receptionist, they could barely hear above the noise of people singing along with an accordion. The desk clerk told them they had the only two rooms in the place not booked by invitees to a wedding scheduled for the next day. Both of them instinctively knew that by Saturday night, after the nuptial reception, the situation would be unbearable. Although they had no alternate plan, Truex said they would not stay. The clerk was delighted to have two more rooms for wedding guests who had arrived unexpectedly.

Campbell drove immediately to Bunny Williams's house to ask if she had any thoughts about where they might find rooms for the weekend. She told them that there wasn't any other place nearby, but they were more than welcome to stay with her. At the time, her house was in the process of being renovated. The walls were bare sheetrock, but the bathrooms were finished, and she had just taken delivery of new mattresses and box springs. If they didn't mind staying in unpainted rooms with no curtains, Williams could offer them beds, a bathroom, and simple food. The kitchen was still under construction. They had to either accept the invitation or return to New York City. They stayed.

Williams remembers that before the real estate agent arrived the following morning, while she and Truex were having coffee in her unfinished kitchen, he asked what color she was going to paint the walls and cabinets. She said she had been thinking about red. "Utterly impossible!" Truex exploded. She recalls being so startled by his dramatic outburst that she nearly jumped out of her seat. With the imperious manner adopted by Charles Le Brun, director of the Manufacture Royale des Meubles de la Couronne under Louis XIV, Truex pronounced that "a kitchen should be one color and one color only: white!" Having issued this dictum, he went on to say that he was disgusted by overdesigned kitchens and outrageously priced appliances that were seldom, if ever, used. A kitchen needed only three things, he insisted: a stove, a sink, and a refrigerator. He then began to enumerate the basic kitchen utensils that were required properly to prepare food. His outpouring of opinions would have continued had Campbell not announced that the real estate agent had arrived for their morning appointment. To this day, Williams has a white kitchen; once Truex delivered his decree, she never dared use anything but white. Remembering that morning, she says, "In my mind, the master had spoken."

During the day, as they looked at properties, Truex felt the pressing re-

ality of the adage "Location, location, location" and the harsh truth of "Compromise" that every home buyer faces. Returning to Williams's home late that
afternoon, he was elated about one house they had seen in the village. Over
dinner in the soon-to-be-white kitchen, Truex described the property in detail. When he asked to be excused and retired early, no one thought it unusual:
everyone who knew Truex was aware that he always went to bed early.

When the realty agent arrived again the next morning, Truex said that
he could not take another full day of looking and would like to be back
at Williams's by midafternoon or earlier. When they returned, at about two
o'clock, their hostess offered them a sandwich, but Truex declined and said he
would like to take a short rest before he and Campbell drove back to the city.
Williams urged them to stay another night and drive home the following day.
Insisting that he had to be in New York early Monday morning, Truex was
definite about leaving that afternoon. Neither Williams nor Campbell
detected his extreme fatigue, and he certainly made no comment about it.
Hoving was the only person who knew about his dire prognosis from the
Mayo Clinic. At about three o'clock, Truex came down from his room in a
fresh outfit and announced that he was ready to leave. He asked Campbell if
he would bring down his bag. Asking for help was something that Truex
never did.

As they drove back to the city, Truex reminisced about his early years in
New York and Paris. Listening to his stories, Campbell was captivated by
Truex's accounts of the years in Paris between the wars. When they got to his
apartment building on East Sixty-third Street, just getting out of the car
seemed to be an effort for Truex. Campbell offered to take his bag upstairs, but
Truex assured him that he could manage with the help of the doorman.
Campbell suggested that they might have an early supper together. Thanking
his young friend for the weekend and for the offer of dinner, Truex said that
he thought he would just have a quiet evening and finish reading the Sunday

New York Times. Although he did not say as much, Truex wanted to have his usual and much-preferred supper, a cup of instant bouillon and a small serving of fruit. He also needed time to think about that house he'd liked in Connecticut; he planned to discuss the finances with John Pierrepont and then make an offer early in the week.

Getting Out of Wisconsin

The earliest records of Van Day Truex's family reveal that early in the seventeenth century, his protestant ancestor Philippe de Trieux, along with his wife, left France and moved to Amsterdam, where the family name was changed to Truex. In 1626, they emigrated with their four sons, Jerome, Abraham, Jacob, and Isaac, to New York City. In New York, Jacob Truex married Elizabeth Joost, who like him was the child of Dutch immigrants. It was to their son, born in New York in 1683, that Van Day Truex's family would trace its origins.

Late in the eighteenth century, Philip's grandson Jacob moved to Pennsylvania. Here his son Benjamin married Catherine Sams. Early in the nineteenth century, Benjamin and Catherine Truex moved to Ohio. Their son Obidiah and his wife, Elizabeth, moved from Ohio to Indiana, where John Morris Truex, Van Day Truex's grandfather, was born. John and his wife, Sarah Ellen, produced nine children, including Truex's father, John Sherman Truex, who was born in Indiana in 1870. Soon after John Sherman's birth, the family moved to Delphos, Kansas.

John Sherman, always known to his family as J.S., following in the tradition of his Truex ancestors, worked on his father's farm. Just before his thirtieth birthday, on February 2, 1900, he married Estel Van Landingham Day, then twenty-four years old, who lived in the neighboring town of Concordia.

Truex, age six, with his two sisters, Phyllis, left, and Mary, 1910.

Both of Estel's parents' families were from Virginia and had been early settlers in Kansas. Her father, Owen Day, owned and operated Van Landingham Hardware, the largest store in the county. After J.S. and Estel's wedding, Owen Day took his daughter's husband into the family hardware business, as his father-in-law had done for him when he married Amanda Van Landingham.

The newly married couple made their first home in Delphos, with J.S. commuting to Concordia for work each day. The 1900 census of Delphos reveals that during their first year of marriage, J.S. and Estel took in a boarder, who was listed in the records without a name, identified only as a "day laborer in the town." The boarder's rent undoubtedly gave the young couple a small additional income. In 1902, J.S and Estel's first child, Phyllis Catherine Truex, was born. On March 5, 1904, Van Day Truex was born. Mary Elizabeth Truex followed in 1906.

In 1908, after eight years of working with his father-in-law, when Van was four, J.S. was hired by J. C. Penney to open his second Golden Rule Store (the name J. C. Penney, Inc., Department Stores would not be used until 1911), in Cumberland, Wyoming. The job had been arranged by Estel's uncle Earl Sams, Penney's right-hand man and a future president of the J. C. Penney Company.

Less than a year later, J.S. and his family moved to Saint Anthony, Idaho, where he opened another Golden Rule Store. Both Cumberland and Saint Anthony were remote towns with populations of fewer than five hundred people. Estel, like the wife of every other Golden Rule Store manager, worked side by side with her husband, helping to tend the store while also making a home for her family. In those early years, Penney's managers, most of whom he also made partners in his business, were poorly paid but generously rewarded with shares of stock in the company. In time, many of them, including J. S. Truex, would become wealthy men.

At the turn of the century, life in isolated western towns had no cul-

tural advantages, and the few schools that existed provided only the most rudi-
mentary education. The fact that endless expanses of western sky and the
Grand Tetons were the only beautiful things that Truex saw in his formative
years helps to explain why he always maintained that nature was the greatest
inspiration for design. One particular incident from his childhood would
come to seem emblematic to him, and he would recall it more than fifty years
later in a lecture he gave at the Wharton School of Business.

According to Truex, one spring day, J. C. Penney came to his father's
store for the annual spring sale, and he offered young Van the job of distribut-
ing handbills throughout the town. During the course of his work, Truex became distracted by some patches of early violets that were blooming along the
roadside. When Penney discovered the boy's negligence, he reprimanded him
severely, saying, "When you work, you work; when you play, you play." While
the admonition would be permanently stamped on Truex's character, the experience did nothing to diminish his fascination with nature. And in the
1950s, after seeing an exhibition of Truex's flower paintings at a gallery in
New York City, Penney would tell him, "Van, you were right. I should have
left you to pick violets."

J. C. Penney purposely located his Golden Rule Stores in rural com-
munities that had no access to retail trade other than catalog sales. The stores
usually consisted of a single ground-floor room in a twenty-by-fifty-foot
wood-frame building. The manager and his family lived in two rooms above
the store. A barn behind the house served as shelter for the family horse and
any other livestock it owned. Neither the store nor the living quarters had
electricity or plumbing; heat was supplied by wood-burning stoves. Water was
brought in from an outside well, and an outdoor privy was the only toilet. The
fire for the family's comfort was lighted only after the store downstairs was
warmed for customers. Enduring these hardships was a way of life for store
managers and their families.

*Estel Truex and John
Sherman Truex
wedding photograph,
1900.*

Winters were brutally hard in the West, especially for young children.
Early in his life, Truex developed a respiratory ailment that would plague him
throughout his years. Living in the poorly heated, often cold rooms above the
Penney stores aggravated his lung condition, and he was often confined to bed
for weeks at a time. His younger sister, Mary, had similar problems and eventually contracted tuberculosis. Phyllis, his older sister, came down with a crip-
pling illness that required her to live the last part of her life in an institution
for disabled persons. Under the strain of these harsh circumstances, Estel gave
birth in 1912 to a second son, Herbert Day Truex. The arrival of his brother
brought a dramatic change in Van Day Truex's life.

Having three sickly children and a new baby was more than Estel could
handle in the family's cramped, miserable living quarters. In those years of financial depression, it was not uncommon for struggling families to send a
child to live with his or her grandparents or some other close relative. For the
Truex family, such an arrangement was a necessity. If one of her children had
to be sent away, Estel believed it should not be either of the girls. She felt

strongly that daughters belonged with their mother, and furthermore, Mary and Phyllis were old enough to help with housework and the baby. Van was therefore the logical one to be sent away. He was then eight years old, and already the deep (and lifelong) rift between him and his father was painfully evident. J.S. relentlessly taunted his son, accusing him of sissyish behavior.

Without any discussion, his father drove Truex to Concordia, Kansas, where he was to live with his great-aunt Puss Van Landingham. His mother's sister, Leta Day Nicol, known as Aunt Kee, had no children and wanted her nephew, whom she adored, to live with her, but unfortunately her husband, Albert Nicol, was also a store manager for J. C. Penney, and their living conditions were no better than the situation young Van was leaving. While he lived in Concordia, Aunt Kee wrote to him every week and regularly sent him money for art supplies. His relationship with her would become a source of considerable jealousy and envy within his family.

When Truex arrived in Concordia, it was no secret to anyone that he was there because his parents were too poor to keep him. His classmates saw his plight as fodder for ridicule. Determined to rise above their badgering, he set it as his goal to be the school's most outstanding student. To accomplish his objective, he developed an extraordinary self-discipline and ended up earning the highest grade in his class. His artistic gifts included a talent for organizing theatrical events. He wrote plays that he also directed and designed the sets and costumes for. While he usually played the lead himself, he also cast his classmates and teachers in supporting roles. These productions added to his growing acceptance.

While Truex was establishing himself among his peers, Aunt Puss was his stalwart champion. A Virginian by birth, she instilled in her young charge the manners of a Southern gentleman. She encouraged his inherent domestic nature, soliciting his help in the kitchen and assigning him the responsibility of setting the dining table for meals. Intrigued by his aesthetic sensibilities, she took pride in his flower arrangements and urged him to use his leisure hours for drawing and painting.

While Truex lived in the comfort of Aunt Puss's home, back in Saint Anthony, Idaho, conditions had not changed for his family. Their long hours of hard work left his parents little time to enjoy life. In fact, the Truex family had few pleasures. Like all Golden Rule Store managers, J.S. opened for business before seven in the morning and often did not close until after midnight. His principles of industry and his striving spirit were deeply imprinted on his elder son's character. J.S. exemplified Penney's requirements for business and personal conduct.

In her book *Creating an American Institution: The Merchandising Genius of J. C. Penney,* the historian Mary Elizabeth Curry records Penney's mandates for members of his organization. In his "Sterling Qualities," Penney stated, "A man of ordinary mind and body and meager attainments inspired and led on by some high ideal accomplishes far more in life than a man with the finest mental, physical strength and splendidly trained, who drifts." Curry further notes that Penney specified that any man who worked for him must "know his business, feel that change is necessary for betterment, be industrious, ambitious, have good habits, and the morals of a Christian." This last dictum definitively excluded Jews from the company. Being reared with this principle as a backdrop could not help but plant questions of ethnicity in Truex's mind.

In 1917, Truex's father moved his family to Rice Lake, Wisconsin, where he opened another Penney store. Here, for the first time, they had a proper house, at 902 Lake Street. J.S. was by then making enough money that Estel no longer had to work in the store and could devote her time to her children. She wrote Aunt Puss that their situation was such that her older son could now rejoin the family. Having lived with Aunt Puss for five years, however, Truex felt that Concordia was his home. In all his time with his great-aunt, he had never told her or anyone else about the revilement he had suffered from his father. When his mother's letter arrived, he begged to stay with Aunt Puss, but she insisted that it would be best for him to be with his own family. Again, his preference about where he was to live was not considered. Having just celebrated his thirteenth birthday, Truex went to Rice Lake.

After five years away, it was not easy for the young teenager to reenter his family. J.S. was more intolerant than ever of his son's effeminate nature, and their conflicts continued. Herbert, then nearly six years old, was a budding athlete and his father's pride and joy. Happiest to have Van home again were Phyllis and Mary, fifteen and eleven, who delighted in their brother's company: he was handsome, he could draw and paint, he wasn't rough like other boys, and he was very smart.

While there is no actual documentation of Truex's intelligence quotient, his academic records clearly show that he ranked at the highest end of the scale. His scholastic transcripts reveal that throughout his schooling, in-

High school graduation day, the Truex family home, Rice Lake, Wisconsin, 1922. Left to right: John Sherman Truex, Estel Truex, Phyllis Truex, Mary Truex (partially visible), Aunt Kee and Uncle Bert Nicol, Van Day Truex. Herbert Truex is in the foreground.

cluding his year of college and his course of study in New York and Paris, he only once received a grade of less than 100. The single exception was a score of 98 on a French exam at Wisconsin State Normal School. In 1922, Truex graduated from Rice Lake High School with highest honors. In each of his years there, he had been president of his class, president of the French Club, and president of the Dramatic Arts Club, which he had founded. His popularity with his peers is evident in the sobriquet printed next to his senior picture in the school yearbook: "A friend to everybody and everybody's friend." Unfortunately, J.S. never saw this side of his son.

One of Truex's cousins in California remembers, "While neither J.S. nor Estel were involved church members, they both subscribed to the prevailing ethic which deemphasized aesthetics, especially on the part of men. In time, J.S. became an active Jehovah's Witness. The teachings of this group served only to intensify his disapproval of Van." J.S. and Estel were not alone

Van Day Truex passport photograph, 1937.

in their criticism of their son. The same cousin recalls that "throughout Van's life everyone in our family always spoke of him with a mixture of pride in his success and disapproval of the way he lived." Truex's only comment about the situation in which he was reared was, "If you wanted to be in the arts in the 1920s, Wisconsin was no place to be."

The impetus that would eventually compel

Truex's exodus and journey east had its origins in the spring of 1922, during his freshman year at Wisconsin State Normal School, now the University of Wisconsin, in Oshkosh. That semester, as in the previous fall term, Truex was scholastically at the top of his class and personally one of the most popular students in the school. When he went in for his adacemic evaluation, his faculty adviser was enthusiastic about his work but raised some questions about his career goals.

When asked about his future plans, Truex said that after graduation he planned to work for the J. C. Penney Company. Explaining that his father was employed there, he said that his parents expected him to continue in the same business. His adviser asked him if he had ever considered a career in art or advertising and went on to say that he and other members of the faculty were impressed with Truex's ability to draw and paint. He pointed out that working for J. C. Penney would undoubtedly preclude Van from using his artistic talents. The academic adviser's remarks were reminiscent of conversations Truex had had with Aunt Puss and Aunt Kee. They both always told him he was cut out to be an artist. At the same time, he was acutely aware that his doing anything related to art would bode serious conflict with his father.

Boosted by his adviser's opinion and confidence, Truex began thinking seriously about a career in advertising. He knew that the training required would mean his having to go to school in Chicago or New York City, since the State Normal School did not offer an art degree. Without sharing any of this with his parents, he sent for several art-school catalogs and after much thought and deliberation applied to the New York School of Fine and Applied Arts. While still in Oshkosh, a few days before the end of the spring term, he received a letter of tentative acceptance. The notification said that final acceptance would be based on a personal interview with the school's president, Frank Alvah Parsons.

Just as Truex had expected, when he told his parents about his plans, they were firmly opposed to the idea. Because he was the first member of his family to attend college, many of his parents' unfulfilled personal ambitions were riding on his earning an academic degree. J.S. so vehemently disapproved of his son's intentions that he said he would not contribute any financial support. When Aunt Kee, who had always been supportive of Truex, heard about her brother-in-law's harsh ultimatum, she agreed to pay for his tuition and room and board. Her generosity only added fuel to his father's wrath, but once Truex had the financial security of Aunt Kee's offer, he was more determined than ever to study art.

The summer before he left for New York City, Truex worked in his father's store in Rice Lake. It was a period of prolonged misery for the entire family. The hours in the store and at home shifted between stretches of agonizing silence and fits of parental rage and anger. By the time that September day finally arrived when Van was to board the train to Chicago, and from there go on to New York City, his relationship with his parents had suffered an irreparable breach.

When he arrived in New York in 1923, the city was even more wondrous than Truex had anticipated. Even walking through the great interior space of Pennsylvania Station was a thrilling experience. While he had read that the station was patterned after the Roman Baths of Caracalla, it was far vaster than he had imagined—though compared to the world he had left behind, *everything* about New York was enormous. Straight from the train, he went to the New York School of Fine and Applied Arts at 2239 Broadway to meet Mr. Parsons. While Parsons's letters had assured him that there would be no problem with his admission, Truex, with his pragmatic nature, was anxious to receive final affirmation of his acceptance.

After Parsons reviewed Truex's transcripts and portfolio, he welcomed the young man as a member of the class of 1926. To Van's amazement, Parsons also said that he was awarding him a full tuition scholarship on the condition that he maintain an A average in all of his courses. Aware that Truex knew no one in the city, Parsons invited him to have dinner with him that evening. Immediately after the interview, Caroline Lanterman, the school secretary, directed Truex to the West Side Branch of the YMCA, at 318 West Fifty-seventh Street, where he would be living. The West Side Y, as it was known, served as a dormitory for most of the male students at the school. In an interview recorded in 1971 for the Smithsonian Archives of American Art, Truex would say, "The Y opened my eyes to many things about life and things about myself that I had always known."

Parsons and His School

Over dinner, well into Truex's first night in New York, Parsons talked about his own life and the history of the New York School of Fine and Applied Arts. Born on April 1, 1868, Parsons had spent his early life in Chesterfield, Massachusetts. After graduating from Wesleyan Seminary, he had spent the next six years traveling and studying art in Italy, France, and England. Then, at the age of thirty-two, he had entered Teachers College, Columbia University. During his two-year course of study there, Parsons had established himself as an original scholar in the decorative arts. Immediately upon his graduation in 1900, he had been asked to join the Columbia faculty.

One of Parsons's first opportunities to lecture outside of Teachers College had come through William Sloane Coffin, a prominent New York businessman and noted philanthropist, who invited him to speak at the West Side Branch of the YMCA. Parsons gave a series of lectures on the use of color, texture, and space in the home. Most of his students at the West Side Y were salesmen at W. & J. Sloane, a prestigious furniture store, which was owned by William Sloane Coffin's family. As the chairman of the Metropolitan Museum of Art, Coffin himself was deeply committed to art and believed passionately in the promotion of the decorative arts through education.

Parsons's friendship with Coffin would prove to be one of his greatest

Truex, upper left, *with three unidentified classmates,*
taken on the steps of the Metropolitan Museum of Art, 1924.

assets. Soon after the YMCA series, Coffin arranged for Parsons to lecture on decorating at the Met, throughout the United States, and in Europe. In addition to being a talented lecturer and teacher, Parsons was a prolific writer. He would produce numerous articles for professional journals and publish six books during his lifetime, including *Interior Decoration: Its Principles and Practice.*

When Parsons talked about the history of the New York School of Fine and Applied Arts, his story rightfully began with William Merritt Chase. Late in the nineteenth century, Chase and a group of fellow so-called progressive artists had become dissatisfied with the conservative attitudes prevalent at the Art Students League. They considered its curriculum decidedly out of date, a poor reflection of the Paris Salon. In 1896, Chase and his followers founded the Chase School of Art. The group envisioned a school that would promote individual expression and the practical application of art in the marketplace. To strengthen his cause, in 1902, Chase incorporated the school as a private institution, owned solely by him, to be known as the New York School of Art.

Two years later, Parsons resigned from his position at Columbia and joined Chase's faculty. Assigned to teach classes in design, color theory, and practical training, he also inaugurated a course of study in interior decoration, the first such curriculum offered by any school in the United States. That same year, his close friend Elsie de Wolfe, then not yet forty, received her first design commission, a milestone that established her as the first professional interior decorator. This was also the year, 1904, that Van Day Truex was born in Delphos, Kansas.

Five years after incorporating the New York School of Art, Chase retired to his home on Long Island, where he could paint without interruption. Parsons, then thirty-nine years old and in his third year on the faculty, negotiated the purchase of Chase's school. In gaining financial control of the institution, Parsons also became the director of all of its educational policies. It was a shift in emphasis that reflected the differences between the two men: whereas Chase was always and foremost a painter, Parsons was ultimately an educator.

In 1909, two years after taking over the reins of authority, Parsons reincorporated the school, again as a private institution, henceforth to be known as the New York School of Fine and Applied Arts. That same year, his star pupil, William Odom, graduated from the school and joined the faculty.

By 1913, enrollment stood at more than twelve hundred students, and the school was generating a considerable profit. In 1920, Parsons and Odom entered into an official business partnership. Odom moved to Paris, where

Frank Alvah Parsons.

he opened the school's first European atelier, at 16 avenue Wagram, near the Arc de Triomphe (a year later, he would relocate it to 9 place des Vosges). Both schools, in New York and Paris, flourished financially. Stanley Barrows, who would join the interior design faculty after World War II and over time become the school's unofficial historian, recalled that Odom and Parsons referred to their annual meeting to share the school's profits, accrued through fees and tuition, as "cutting up the melon."

From the very beginning, Frank Alvah Parsons was recognized by most educators as being a brilliant teacher and administrator. He also had the reputation of being able to attract an impressive roster of visiting critics, the foremost authorities in their fields. As early as 1917, he hired Miriam Smyth, future head of the prestigious decorating firm Smyth, Urquhart & Marckwald, to be the assistant director of the Department of Interior Design. That same year, Elsie de Wolfe, Elsie Cobb Wilson, and Lady Duff Gordon (known in the world of fashion as Lucille) were listed as members of the advisory board. In 1922, Francis Lenygon, the noted interior designer of many of the great houses of England, and Heyworth Campbell, the art director of *Vogue,* joined the board. Eleanor McMillen (later Brown) and Ogden Codman, Jr., likewise served as advisers to the school for many years.

An archconservative in aesthetic matters, Parsons had a deep aversion to the new art that emerged from Europe in the first decades of the twentieth century. Even before the Armory Show of 1913, he disliked all modern painting, architecture, design, sculpture, and music. He thought it absurd that the avant-garde artists ignored the importance of the past, especially eighteenth-century and neoclassical design. While the majority of Americans agreed with him, there were a few with money, power, and influence who became patrons of the new order. In 1929, Abby Aldrich Rockefeller, Mary Quinn Sullivan, and Lillie P. Bliss would found the Museum of Modern Art; ten years later, Solomon R. Guggenheim would open his Museum of Non-Objective Art. Neither of these museums or its collections would interest Parsons. For him, Style Moderne (later, in its 1960s revival, to be called art deco), which permeated American fashion, Hollywood set designs, and New York skyscrapers after the 1925 Paris Exposition, was anathema. Even after the spire of William Van Allen's Chrysler Building rose to dominate the New York skyline (making it, for a brief time, the tallest building in the world), Parsons would dismiss art deco as a passing fancy, to be ignored in the same way he had earlier disregarded the Arts and Crafts movement and art nouveau.

Neither was the work of Frank Lloyd Wright (then America's only modern architect) or Le Corbusier's emerging modernism ever formally discussed at the school. Parsons considered eighteenth-century French and English Georgian design the ultimate styles, if not the only styles worth acknowledging, in architecture and interior decoration. His attitude reflected the opinion of most of America's rich and powerful, who continued to commission designs from architects such as Mott B. Schmidt, William Adams Delano, and John Russell Pope.

Although the school never actually offered courses in architecture, Parsons was totally committed to emulating the program of study at the École des Beaux-Arts. Throughout his tenure, he would emphasize the study of antiquities, the Italian Renaissance, eighteenth-century French architecture and decorative arts, and the neoclassical tradition. Academic subjects such as mathematics, the humanities, and languages were not taught at the school; instead, the curriculum focused on applied arts and how they related to specific products and to the job market. Parsons was well aware that his method of teaching drew criticism from other educators. According to Truex, "From the beginning the school never pretended to offer the technical training given at Pratt, Cooper Union, or the Rhode Island School of Design. These were all wonderful schools, but we never offered more than a little of what these schools called practical courses. In the three years that the students were at our school, the objective was to train their eye, instill in them an idea of quality, and develop their sense of style."

All students were required to take life drawing classes, which met all day every Saturday. Art history lectures were supplemented by field trips to the Metropolitan Museum of Art. During their first year, students also took a two-semester course entitled "Dynamic Symmetry." Taught by Parsons himself, it was based on the canon of proportion developed by the late Jay Hambidge, who had posited that space was relative to design, just as harmony was to music. Hambidge's theory, taken from Egyptian and classical Greek design, was supported by a series of triangles and their perpendiculars, which in turn yielded the "root rectangles." The complexity and rigor of the Hambidge principles have kept the canon from being widely taught, but it remains a useful system for any artist or designer interested in creating compositions that will appeal to a viewer's unconscious sense of proportion. For Parsons, dynamic symmetry was the basis of all good design.

By 1923, more than sixty specialized schools and hundreds of colleges in the United States offered courses in interior decoration, costume and fashion design, fashion illustration, and advertising design. Under Parsons's leadership, the New York School of Fine and Applied Arts was recognized as having the finest programs in the country. He fostered the mystique that being admitted to the school was a distinct privilege, and promoted what Truex described as a "marked degree of snobbery." In 1971, Truex would say that even though the school had been accused of "turning out dilettantes," the elitist attitude that had originated with Parsons seemed to him "all to the good."

When Truex entered the school, an interview with Parsons was the only real requirement for admission. While this might appear to be a benevolent test, it most definitely was not. Parsons had firm ideas about who was to be admitted to the New York School of Fine and Applied Arts, boasting that only the most talented students were allowed to attend, and maintaining that any person who graduated left with the potential to be the best in his or her field. Parsons expected every student to exhibit talent and to possess a solid secondary education. His chief concern when it came to women, then referred to as "girls," was their social credentials: Parsons wanted them to be proper young ladies from elite families. Many of them were driven around in chauffeured limousines, arriving at the school in designer outfits and fur coats. Egalitarian it was not: when the sister of one of the school's graduates enrolled to study fashion design, she was so intimidated by the snobbish attitude that she left before the end of her first semester and transferred to a less pressured school in the Midwest.

Melvin Dwork, a leading New York decorator, and Jay Hyde Crawford, one of America's legendary fashion illustrators, both remember that when they attended the school, just after World War II, the Frank Alvah Parsons mystique was still very much in evidence. The idea that it was the *best* school, to which only the *most* talented applicants were admitted, clearly presisted. Both Dwork and Crawford recall that they and the other students were soberly and soundly conditioned to believe that it was a distinct honor for them to be there. A prominent New York advertising executive remembers that in 1950, after being enrolled for only a few weeks, he was called into the president's office, where Truex (then the school's head) politely informed him that after much consideration, the faculty had decided he should withdraw. When he asked why he was being dismissed, he was told, "You do not fit into the program." He relates that while it was not a comfortable experience for him, he knew Truex was right. He explains, "I was something of a wise-cracker. I had the talent but I didn't have the polish that was required."

When Truex entered the school, not only did he meet all of Parsons's basic requirements for admission, but he was the epitome of the man's expectations. Having grown to his full height, Truex was nearly six foot three. He was extremely thin, with amazingly erect posture, patrician features, an appealing, square-set jaw, and crystal-blue eyes. If he had any feature that was less than flattering, it was his protruding ears, but he would soon learn to groom his thick blond hair so as to cover this slight mischance of nature. In addition to taking responsibility for Truex's academic training, Parsons became his social mentor. He nurtured him in the manners and mores of New York society, tutored him in the art of conversation, and frequently took him along to parties, where he introduced his young liege as the school's most promising student. One of Truex's classmates remembers, "From the first day of classes, it was obvious to everyone that Van was Mr. Parsons's prodigy." Not since William Odom entered the school had Parsons found such delight in one of his students.

Odom

William MacDougall Odom, or "Mr. Taste," as he is remembered, was born on May 30, 1884, in Columbus, Georgia. In 1906, he moved to New York to study music with Leopold Stokowski, but because of a back injury incurred in childhood, he found himself unable to sit for the long hours of keyboard practice required. Stokowski encouraged him to study commercial art, a vocation that would impose less physical strain. Odom applied to the New York School of Fine and Applied Arts and was accepted into the class that would be the first to graduate under Frank Alvah Parsons's administration. During his three years at the school, Odom never matriculated as a regular student. For him, Parsons designed individual courses in architecture and the decorative arts that demanded extended travel in France, Italy, and England. Parsons himself frequently accompanied Odom on these trips abroad.

From the beginning, Odom and Parsons had a connection that extended beyond the realm of academics. Their relationship of student and teacher would be repeated between Truex and Parsons and then between Truex and Odom. The association that Odom had with Parsons, and Truex's relationship with each of them, in some ways resembled the bond between an adoring son and a benevolent father. These alliances no doubt gave both Odom and Truex a sense of paternal affirmation that neither of them had ex-

William Odom.

perienced with his own father. Odom's father, a fiercely masculine horse trainer, had once bullied him into taking a jump on a horse that had resulted in his being seriously injured. The accident had caused a breach so deep, and so final, that Odom would later erase all references to his father in every account of his life.

Upon Odom's graduation, in 1909, Parsons made him a member of the interior decorating faculty, and a year later promoted him to head of the department. Each summer from then until 1914, Odom conducted a six-week study tour of France and Italy that was extremely popular with the students. The young women who went on these trips were customarily accompanied by either their mothers or chaperons. Odom used the time abroad to establish himself among the most important, influential, and wealthy people in the capitals of Europe. In 1920, Parsons offered him a business partnership contingent upon his setting up a European branch of the school. With ready entrée to the inner sanctum of French society, Odom agreed to open a Paris offshoot of the New York School of Fine and Applied Arts.

The Paris school's first address, 16 avenue Wagram, near the Etoile, lacked both the space and the distinction that Odom wanted, and after a year he moved it to 9 place des Vosges. Today the site is occupied by the prestigious Michelin three-star restaurant L'Ambroisie. Here, in the heart of the Marais, on what Parisians and visitors alike consider the most beautiful residential square in the world, Odom set up his new offices and classrooms. In Odom's persuasive words, "[The school,] in the ancient Hôtel de Chaulnes, contains one of the most precious Louis XVI rooms in Paris and is replete with interesting paneling, old chimney pieces, and other decorative features. The ateliers, which will accommodate at least two hundred students, provide comfortable and efficient facilities and in the immediate vicinity are the Musée Carnavalet, the ancient Hôtel Soubise, and many of the most beautiful old houses of Paris. Within a ten-minute walk [are] the Louvre, the Musée des Arts Décoratifs, and the Palais Royal."

The Paris school offered both a twelve-week summer program and a full academic year of study, with classes taught in a manner similar to that used in the New York school, but supplemented with supervised and highly disciplined study at museums and historic houses. The curriculum reflected Odom's adamant belief that "in all enlightened social epochs the recognition of classical law and order, governing both life and its expression, has been of paramount importance." He supported his opinions with facts, pointing out that the French Academy in Rome had been founded during the reign of Louis XIV; that Francis I and the Medici queens had relied on Rome for the underlying principles of the arts and architecture of France; and that Inigo Jones and Christopher Wren had overcome "illiteracy in the arts in eighteenth-century England through their recognition of the classical traditions and opened the way for English classic revival." Finally, Odom cited the example of the Adam brothers, who had spent the greater part of their time in Italy measuring classical ruins, an investigation that would later enable them to create "one of the most original styles of architecture and decoration in England." On these principles, Odom successfully launched a unique program that would set the standard for studies in the decorative arts.

Early on in the venture, Odom invited the social elite of Paris and the circle of wealthy American expatriates to be the patrons of the school. Miss Elsie de Wolfe; Mrs. William K. Vanderbilt; Walter Gay, the celebrated painter of interiors; and Mrs. Edith Wharton and her coauthor of *The Decoration of Houses,* the architect Ogden Codman, Jr., were among the Americans living in Paris who backed Odom in his new school. Being a devout Episcopalian, Odom also asked the Very Reverend Frederick Beekman, dean of the Episcopal Cathedral of the Holy Trinity, to join his board of advisers. Informally referred to as the American Cathedral, the church had been built in 1896, with monies donated by J. P. Morgan, to serve as the parish home of Episcopalians in Paris. Immediately after World War I and throughout the twenties and thirties, it would be the favored gathering place of wealthy and influential Americans. Getting Dean Beekman to sit on his board was a major coup for Odom. Once the Paris school was established, Odom inaugurated field studies and travel programs in London, Rome, Florence, and Venice, in which cities he was no less effective in gaining the support of rich Americans and Europeans for his endeavors.

While still a student, on one of his first trips to Europe, Odom had met Paul Chalfin, the highly respected art and antiques buyer who was then working for the American millionaire James Deering. Although Odom was only twenty-four, Chalfin hired him to assist in the purchase of art, furniture, and architectural details for Deering's Italianate mansion, Vizcaya, in Miami, Florida. The reputation Odom earned through his work on the Vizcaya project resulted in his subsequently being hired as the European agent for several other wealthy Americans and prominent decorators. One of his earliest clients was Myron Taylor, the chairman of U.S. Steel and a future ambassador to the Vatican. Odom acquired all the furnishings for both Taylor's palatial house in Florence and his estate on Long Island. Throughout his years as director of the Paris school, Odom would continue diligently to supply antiques for his clients. Some supporters of the school would criticize his commercial enterprise and view it as a conflict of interest, but there is no evidence that the school suffered because of it. The enormous sums that Odom earned on his commissions allowed him to enjoy an opulent life-style that included a chauffeur-driven Rolls-Royce, a palazzo in Florence, a house in London and one on Long Island, an apartment in Paris, and a suite at the St. Regis Hotel in New York City.

Eleanor Brown would always give Odom credit for suggesting that she open her own decorating firm, McMillen, Inc., and from the beginning he was her European antiques buyer. The pleasure and satisfaction that Mrs. Brown derived from their association fostered her total allegiance to Odom and the school. Without reservation, she trusted his every decision, and once said of him, "The man could not place a book on a table that it did not look special." It didn't matter to Mrs. Brown that he was extravagant and a social snob; for her, the important things were his judgment and taste. Odom accepted the affirmation of Mrs. Brown, and others whom he respected, as the rightful acknowledgment of self-evident truths. This sense of confidence would be one of his greatest gifts to Truex, and Truex would wear it well. Billy Baldwin, who always coveted Truex's approval of his work, would say jestingly, "You know, in everything Van thinks he has perfect taste. Whatever that means!" Echoing Baldwin's affectionate gibe, an executive at Tiffany & Company recalls, "At Tiffany's, there were two ways of doing things: the wrong way, and Truex's way, which was perfect. At least *he* thought so. In fact, we all agreed."

Odom secured his reputation as an expert in period furniture when, in 1918, he published his two-volume *History of Italian Furniture.* The book, reissued in 1966, remains an authoritative reference on design and decoration. In recognition of his achievements in advancing the decorative arts in France, he was made a Chevalier de la Légion d'Honneur. While Frank Alvah Parsons is today the more widely known of the two men, thanks to the Parsons School of Design, William Odom is the one remembered—and still revered—in the world of interior design.

The Student Years in New York and Paris

*T*here is no indication that after his arrival in New York City in 1923, Truex ever doubted his decision to oppose his parents and enroll at the New York School of Fine and Applied Arts. His inner strength and his resolve never to look back were always two of his greatest assets. At the time, the J. C. Penney Company maintained a buying division in New York City, which could have provided a measure of security for a young man so far from home—but young Truex had been told by his father that under no circumstances was he to contact the Penney office. The edict loomed as a further indication of his parents' disapproval of his decision to study art. Their attitude, however, never discouraged him in the slightest: the experience of being completely alone in the biggest city in the world was in no way as intimidating as the deprecating environment Truex had managed to escape.

While Truex had never before been in the East, some of his earliest memories were of his father's disgruntled stories about his annual buying trips in the great metropolis. J. S. Truex always said that leaving New York was the smartest thing his ancestors had ever done. He hated everything about the place—the crowds, the hurried pace, the bright lights, the tall buildings. All of the things he most disliked about New York City were the things his son yearned to experience.

Watercolor rendering by Truex, done in Paris, 1925.

The Armistice celebration, heralding victory and the end of the Great War, had occurred five years before Van Day Truex came to New York, but in 1923 the city was still in exuberant spirits. From the hour the returning doughboys marched down Fifth Avenue, New York was seized by a euphoria that would not subside until Wall Street crashed in 1929. When the Armistice parade ended, the pounding drums and blasting bugles, without missing a beat and in close syncopation, caught the upswing of a new sound called jazz. An ever-present madcap atmosphere magnified New York's fabled life of sex and glamour. The Charleston, and the short dresses that accompanied it, signaled not only a new freedom in women's fashion but also a new style of living. The talk in the city was all about money; the drink of choice was bonded bootleg whiskey. The delirium was heightened by the deafening din emanating from the construction of skyscrapers, modern-day wonders that were rising like steel behemoths across the southern tip of Manhattan. With silly abandon, people sang "Way Down Yonder in New Orleans" and "Nothin' Could Be Finer Than to Be in Carolina"—but for Truex, New York City was the best place to be. His youthful enthusiasm and sense of adventure are reflected in his face in snapshots made soon after his arrival, which clearly indicate that he was caught up in the spirit of that year's hit song, "Ain't We Got Fun."

Truex's elected program of study was listed in the school catalog as Advertising Art. Frank Alvah Parsons specified that the purpose of the course was "to produce art work in which one has an idea to sell." Each student was expected to "develop a selective eye for creating a picture and fitting that image to accurate and economical reproduction." To accomplish that objective, the students were required to study layout, composition, rendering, poster advertising, commercial design, and costume illustration. Their core curriculum also included lettering and both freehand and mechanical drawing.

Museum field trips for specific research projects were an integral part of students' assignments. Frequently an entire class would spend several consecutive days working in the galleries of the Metropolitan Museum. In the twenties, museums were dimly lit, dusty corridors where the students could sketch or paint with no interruption other than the occasional passing of a security guard. In addition to the required fieldwork, Truex did research at the American Museum of Natural History, which furthered his knowledge and love of nature in design. Both in the school's supervised drawing classes and working on his own, he produced prodigious architectural renderings. The first drawings that Truex did at the school were remarkably competent, given that he had had no previous art training. His eye for simplicity and his innate ability to delete unnecessary details distinguished him as the most exceptional student in the school.

During his first semester, Truex developed a camaraderie with a second-year student named Adrian Greenburg. Their friendship, which would last for the next fifty years, was enhanced by their shared fascination with drawing animals, and the two men spent long hours that year sketching together at the Bronx Zoo. Before he left New York in 1924 for Paris, where he was to finish his course of study, Greenburg changed his name to Gilbert Adrian. Less than a year later, when he graduated and his meritorious career in costume design was launched, he would be known to the world as Adrian.

Truex also had an innate ability to teach, and he quickly became a self-appointed tutor to his fellow students. Whenever he encountered someone struggling with a problem in perspective, applying an ink wash, or trying to capture the essence of a drawing assignment, Truex readily gave assistance. Parsons and members of his faculty were unreserved in their admiration of the young man's talents. A less ambitious personality could easily have coasted in such favored circumstances, but any semblance of indolence was foreign to Truex's nature.

When his first year ended, in 1924, Truex had earned the academic dis-

Black-and-white drawing done by Truex at Fontainebleau, 1925. Labeled by him "My first wash drawing in France."

tinction of being the top student in his class. At the close of the second semester, Parsons offered him a summer bursary job in the school library. Throughout the summer months, Truex used his free time after work and on weekends to draw and paint, spending endless hours sketching at the Metropolitan Museum and the American Museum of Natural History. Many young women enrolled at the school came from families that had summer houses in Connecticut or on Long Island, and on several occasions, Truex was invited to join them and their friends for weekends in the country. Through these invitations and the social introductions that Parsons had arranged for him during the school term, he was gaining entrance to a very privileged world. Eleanor McMillen, a recent graduate of the school and a close friend of Parsons's, frequently asked Truex to join her for meals. This was the beginning of one of the most important friendships and professional connections of his life. The summer recess also gave him the freedom to explore New York City on his own: without the restraints imposed on his social life by Parsons, he could explore the Village, frequent the jazz clubs of Harlem, and establish his own priorities.

In September 1924, at the beginning of his second academic year, Truex rented a fourth-floor room in a boardinghouse on Waverly Place in Greenwich Village. In a 1971 interview, he would describe his landlady, Mrs.

Remington (sister-in-law of the American artist Frederick Remington), as a "strange woman who wore long black satin dresses, tied her hair in a red bandana, and kept psychic cats." He went on to say, "That was in the days, you see, when the Village was the real place."

When classes reconvened, Parsons resumed his dominant role in Truex's life. Even though their relationship placed demands and constrictions on him, from Parsons Truex received an acceptance and assurance that he had never before known. The beginning of the term also rekindled the constant pressure on him to excell in his studies. Ever before him was the sobering reality that his scholarship was dependent on his continuing academic achievement.

The second-year Advertising Art course was basically a continuation of the work that had begun the year before, with an increased emphasis on historical research. Truex's summer job in the library had given him broad exposure to the school's resources, which proved to be a distinct advantage in every assignment.

Parsons and the faculty encouraged him to pursue independent study projects. Late in the spring term, Parsons arranged for him to meet with Elsie de Wolfe. Before the meeting, Parsons confided to de Wolfe that Truex was being considered for a Paris scholarship and said he would appreciate hearing her opinion on the young man and his work.

The fact that Truex was extremely svelte unquestionably made a good first impression on de Wolfe. According to Ludwig Bemelmans, writing in his book *La Bonne Table,* she preferred men and dogs who were thin. Truex also had a knack for wearing clothes well. He had come away from seeing the musical *Lady Be Good* captivated by Fred Astaire's sartorial flair and dreaming of having the dancer's panache and wearing custom-tailored suits like his. While he did not have the money for such luxury at the time, he had a reputation for being able to give style to a seersucker jacket, khaki pants, and a pair of sneakers. Elsie de Wolfe was fascinated by him. After seeing his portfolio, the decorator reported to Parsons that she had never met a man so young with such charm, talent, and promise. Her praise was music to Parsons's ears; Truex, after all, was the product of his own making. Truex himself would never forget that when Parsons summoned him into his office to announce that he had been awarded the Paris scholarship, he ended the conversation by advising, "It would be wise for you to make no further reference about your being from Kansas."

When Truex wrote to tell Aunt Kee that he had been selected to study in France, she agreed to help with his finances. Any joy she might have taken in his accomplishments, however, was far outweighed by her anxiety and concerns over his future. She had fears about someone so young, with so little worldly experience, living in Paris. While he had written regularly to her, she could not imagine how much maturity Truex had gained in the two years since she had last seen him. Her greatest worry was that the year in Paris would further lessen any hope of reconciliation between her nephew and his parents.

Even with the tuition scholarship and Aunt Kee's help, Truex still lacked sufficient funds for the trip. He also had reservations about not spending his senior year at the New York school. Over the past two years, he had come to depend on Parsons's companionship and guidance, and the older man's personal approval had become a motivating force in his life. At this critical juncture, William Odom would come to Truex's financial and emotional aid.

On visits to the New York school during the two previous years, Odom had met Truex and noted Parsons's possessive attitude toward him. Not wanting to offend Parsons, Odom had maintained a distant, though cordial, formality with the young student. When he was informed that Parsons had awarded Truex the Paris scholarship, and learned of his financial difficulties, he wrote and offered him a job as his chauffeur. Odom's letter indicated that he, like Parsons, was well aware of Truex's sensitivities and abilities. The letter gave Truex the assurance he needed. As he prepared to leave New York City in 1925, the hoi polloi was enthralled with the golden age of Broadway. Infused with the spirit of the year's hit songs, "I'm Sitting on Top of the World" and "I Want to Be Happy," Truex was off to Paris.

Social and political unrest, some of it the result of Americans' living high on the inflated U.S. dollar and Parisians' barely getting by on the falling French franc, greeted Truex on his landing in France. While he did not have much money, the little he had went a long way. His fluent French was also an asset. The welcome he received from William Odom, his new mentor, was beyond his expectations. When Truex arrived at 9 place des Vosges, he found Odom's demeanor decidedly different from that of the somewhat aloof man he had met in New York. Although small and delicately built, Odom had a commanding and assertive presence. Years later, when Truex reminisced about that time in France, he never failed to tell about the first and only day he worked as Odom's chauffeur. According to Truex, after a morning of shopping for antiques, he and Odom stopped for lunch at a restaurant outside Paris. Following an afternoon of prolonged conviviality, Odom arranged for another driver to take them back into the city, and he and Truex rode home together in the backseat. After this propitious outing, Truex never again worked as Odom's chauffeur.

As Parsons had done in New York, Odom now dominated Truex's life, maintaining complete control over both his academic and his social schedules. Truex, then and always, revered his new mentor as a paragon of knowledge and taste. The first thing Odom did for his new scholar was to kindle, deep within him, a passionate love of French and Italian architecture and antiques. Under Odom's tutelage, Truex would develop a remarkable eye for even the subtlest details of eighteenth-century design.

One of the many privileges enjoyed by students at the Paris school in the 1920s was being invited to the spring and fall openings of the Paris fashion designers Paul Poiret, Madeleine Vionnet, and Alix Grès. They also had the advantage of attending exclusive lectures and drawing classes at the Louvre, the Musée Carnavalet, Versailles et les Trianons, and the Palais de Compiègne. On such field trips, each student was required to take precise measurements of eighteenth-century *boiserie* and furniture and record them in meticulously rendered drawings. Beyond these field trips for the entire class, Truex was accorded certain exclusive privileges. Through introductions arranged by Odom, he gained entrée to many of the great private houses of Paris, where he could see and examine some of the finest furniture, porcelain, and fabrics of *le grand siècle.* These excursions had the added bonus of giving him social exposure to the influential and socially prominent people who owned or occupied the houses and châteaux, including Comte Etienne de Beaumont and Prince Jean-Louis de Faucigny-Lucinge.

When Truex arrived in Paris, all of the arts—painting, music, sculpture, writing, and photography—were pulsing with an energy and creativity that reflected the political and social unrest of the era, as well as its rapidly emerging new technologies. This phenomenon had begun in 1909, when Parisians first saw the designs of Léon Bakst in the Russian aristocrat Sergei Diaghilev's productions for the Ballets Russes. Cecil Beaton described Diaghilev as "one of the baker's dozen of powerful personalities who have helped to foster the arts since Renaissance individualism."

By 1925, Truex's first year in the city, the cubist movement was in full flower in Paris. The ghetto of avant-garde artists had moved from Montmartre to the Left Bank, finding refuge in the neighborhoods of Montparnasse and St.-Germain-des-Prés. While Truex would live in this area from 1925 until 1939, there is no indication in his collection of photographs that he was ever part of this group of artists. In an interview in 1971, he would recall, "I was there in the days of the beginning of the brilliant Paris school of painting, you know, Picasso and Braque, but as students we were not made aware of this. Odom never took much interest in the contemporary world. I went out with the first money I had and bought a pair of bastard candelabra with purple crystal drops hanging off them. I mean ghastly. Had I known more I could have bought a small but important painting for the same amount of money in 1927. I must admit that we were never directed in the contemporary scene, except, of course we did see the big expositions."

In the autumn of 1925, the biggest event in Paris was the Exposition Internationale des Arts Décoratifs et Industriels Modernes, the first and last world exposition devoted entirely to the decorative arts. The French exhibits displayed the crowning glories of Style Moderne (later to be known as art deco) and announced to the world that once again Paris, not Vienna, was the center of the decorative arts. Since the Vienna Congress Exhibit of 1896 and the formation of the Wiener Werkstätte in 1903, the French had chafed under the knowledge that they had been surpassed in the world of art and design. The Great War had forced France to delay an exhibition, planned for 1917, that would reclaim her supreme position. Now, in 1925, the glory of France once again reigned.

The exposition covered seventy-five acres from the Invalides, across the Seine, to the Grand Palais. The two hundred buildings that comprised the exposition were filled with displays from seventeen countries, a number of leading manufacturers, and the large Paris department stores. Germany was not included for political reasons. The guiding premise was that each exhibitor was to show only new work that did not rely on previous designs. Herbert Hoover, then secretary of Commerce under President Calvin Coolidge, said the United States would not be represented because it had nothing new to show.

The star of the exposition was Emile-Jacques Ruhlmann, who displayed his elaborate furniture in magnificent interiors. All of the major Paris designers followed Ruhlmann's lead, showing luxurious objects and furniture so costly that only the wealthiest clients could afford them. This attitude was closer to the exclusivity of the eighteenth century than to the modern notion that art and design should be available to all. As a result, many, if not most, critics felt that the exposition failed to achieve its original purpose. Despite such opinions, Ruhlmann's aesthetic had a powerful influence on Truex, as would become evident thirty years later in his work for Tiffany & Company. Photographs of Truex's Paris apartments, meanwhile, made between 1925 and 1939, reveal that he was reluctant to venture far from Odom's tether.

The one exception to the extravagant displays by Ruhlmann and others of his design persuasion was the exhibit of the Jeanneret cousins, Charles-Edouard (Le Corbusier) and Pierre. Their pavilion, l'Esprit Nouveau, named for the journal they published, was constructed of the simplest materials and outfitted with machine-made furniture. Unfortunately, l'Esprit Nouveau was poorly located within the exhibit area, and most of those who bothered to seek it out were not favorably impressed. It was, in fact, not even mentioned in the American and English guidebooks to the exposition. But unpopular though it might have been, the exhibit clearly signaled the beginning of modernism and a new age of design.

On March 29, 1926, during the spring semester of Truex's senior year, Elsie de Wolfe married Sir Charles Mendl. While she would continue to be known professionally as Elsie de Wolfe, in social situations she preferred the title Lady Mendl. Like Parsons, Odom considered Lady Mendl a close friend, unaware that *she* found *him* quite boring at times and had little interest in his erudite conversation. While she liked fine antiques, she was not obsessed with them; her real interest lay in selling them to wealthy clients. Her Paris apartment and her house in Versailles, Villa Trianon, were beautifully furnished, but the antiques therein were by no means museum pieces. Never an intellectual, Lady Mendl nonetheless had a genius for show business, for creating the effect

Truex snapshots of a Sunday afternoon at Villa Trianon, Versailles, 1938.
Clockwise from top left: Kitty Miller and Bernard Boutet de Monvel; dining
room; Elsa Schiaparelli with Cole Porter; Mrs. Wellington Koo, wife of the Chinese
ambassador to Great Britain, and Sir Charles Mendl (with back to camera); Lady
Mendl (Elsie de Wolfe).

*Mary Rogers, Senlis,
France, 1925.*

of luxury; she was at her best when recapturing the spirit of Percier and Fontaine in her striped, tented rooms.

Lady Mendl assumed complete credit for Truex's winning the Paris scholarship, and on occasion she invited him, without Odom, to visit her at Villa Trianon. But from the beginning of his days in Paris, Truex was careful never completely to restrict himself to the worlds of William Odom and Lady Mendl. Early in the fall of 1925, he started visiting the workrooms of the leading Paris decorators. One of the firms that fascinated him was owned by the designers Louis Süe and André Mare, who were responsible for much of the Paris exhibition. It was at their atelier that Truex first met Bernard Boutet de Monvel, who was engaged in painting murals for the firm. Intrigued by the inquisitive young student, Boutet asked to see his portfolio, and after reviewing Truex's work, he labeled him a "serious artist untainted by fashion." Their chance meeting marked the beginning of a friendship that would last for more than twenty years. Boutet soon began including Truex in small social gatherings. The first people he introduced him to were Mary Benjamin Rogers, first wife of the Standard Oil millionaire Henry Huttleston Rogers, Jr., and her daughter, Millicent, then married to the Austrian count Ludwig von Salm-Hoogstraten.

From the moment Mary Rogers met Truex, she unabashedly loved him as a surrogate son. H. H. Rogers III, her natural son, had always been a sad disappointment to her, beset as he was by a serious drinking problem and a life of scandal that had virtually alienated him from both of his parents. Truex was Mary Rogers's ideal. Her grandson Paul Peralta-Ramos remembers, "Van was all that she had wanted her son to be. In her mind he was perfect. Van was so much a part of our life that he even called my brother, Arturo, Brother. This pet name was reserved only for members of our family." Millicent, too, was captivated by Truex. As her older son, Arturo Peralta-Ramos, recalls, "By the time our mother and father were married in 1927, and certainly before I was born in 1928 and Paul in 1932, Van was already accepted as one of the family. He and Mother had a unique friendship. She was devoted to him." Realizing that Truex had little money, Mary and Millicent both made sure that he never wanted for anything. Neither of them saw this as charity; for Mary Rogers, giving money to Truex was the same as taking care of her own children.

On one of Truex's frequent visits to Rogers's country house in Senlis, he was introduced to the fashion designer Madame Elsa Schiaparelli. Truex and Schiaparelli liked each other and shared an understanding of hard work

and determination. They were both driven by a fierce discipline that had allowed them to over-come their early exposure to deprivation. Truex became a regular visitor at Schiaparelli's apartment, where he met the avant-garde of Paris. It was there that he first encountered Sal-vador Dalí. Truex's social world was soon spinning well beyond William Odom's conservative orbit.

Soon after Dalí was in-troduced to Truex, he presented him with one of his paintings, *Decor for the Ballet "Labyrinth."*

Millicent Rogers, seated above, with her mother, Mary Rogers. Taken by Truex at Claremont, Millicent Rogers's Tidewater, Virginia, estate, 1943.

To create a background for this Surrealist canvas, Truex completely redecorated his Left Bank flat. Wanting to emulate the look of Lady Mendl's tented salon at Villa Trianon, but working on a small budget, he covered the walls and ceilings with striped mattress ticking. This example of Truex's natural flair recalls the creativity of another of Schiaparelli's young protégés, Jean Schlumberger, who early on in his career used discarded porcelain funeral flowers, collected from cemeteries in and around Paris, to make buttons for Schiaparelli's jackets and costume jewelry. The whimsy that both Schlumberger and Truex displayed in their work was emblematic of the kind of imagination that fascinated Schiaparelli.

It was also through Schiaparelli, in 1936, that Truex met Pauline Potter. Having recently abandoned her first husband, Fulton Leser, in Spain, she had reclaimed her family name and was working in Schiaparelli's boutiques in London and Paris. At the time, Potter had little money, and her life was filled with difficulty and insecurity. She had spent part of her early life in Baltimore, Maryland, where one of her closest friends was the interior decorator Billy Baldwin. Although Truex and Baldwin would not meet until 1939, Potter paved the way for the two men's future friendship. Even many years later, after Potter became the wife of the wealthy and much-publicized Baron Philippe de Rothschild, she and Truex would remain close.

Of all of Schiaparelli's friends, the one who most intrigued Truex was Jean-Michel Frank. When the two men first met, Frank questioned the whole notion of studying interior decorating in a school. He believed that decorating was a trade one learned from apprenticeship to the masters, not something that could be taught in a classroom. Certainly he could not imagine that an American school could have much to offer the French in either fashion or the decorative arts. Not long after their initial encounter, in 1926, Frank returned to Italy, and Truex went back to New York City. Fortunately, they would meet again.

In 1926, Truex graduated from the New York School of Fine and Applied Arts in Paris. His academic performance and his teaching abilities prompted Parsons to offer him a position on the faculty. Flattered though he was by the proposal, Truex had one serious reservation: Parsons wanted him to teach in Manhattan, and after living in Paris, he viewed New York as an unrefined city, where the only thing that mattered was money. In his opinion, New Yorkers, like most Americans in 1926, were living in a bubble of fantasy that was reflected in the absurd lyrics of popular songs such as "Baby Face," "When the Red, Red Robin Comes Bob, Bob, Bobbin' Along," and "Bye Bye Blackbird." Paris was also where his closest friends lived. While Odom was sympathetic, he urged Truex to accept Parsons's offer, promising to arrange for him to return to the Paris school the following year.

Having saved the money given him by Mary Rogers, Truex had sufficient funds to stay in Paris for the summer. As usual, Odom was summering in England and offered his young protégé the use of his flat. On weekends, Truex went with friends to the Loire Valley or the Normandy coast, outings that provided some relief from the oppressive heat of Paris and the agonizing thought of having to leave France. In late August, he packed up his few things, including his Dalí painting, and sailed for New York.

When classes started in New York that September, Parsons's interest in Truex had diminished not at all. This was evident to the faculty when he was made an "instructor," not an "assistant," in graphic advertising and illustration. Throughout the academic year of 1926–1927, Truex enjoyed a great rapport with the students. Close to their age, he had an affinity for their lives and was sympathetic to their problems. Most faculty members maintained an aloof attitude toward the students; the prevailing philosophy at the school was "You have come here to learn. Forget everything you thought you knew. Do exactly as you are told. Speak only when spoken to." Truex was far more open to the students' ideas and genuinely wanted to hear what they had to say. By listening to them, Truex gained their respect and admiration. Not only was he Parsons's prize faculty member; he was the pride of the student body.

Truex always made lengthy, thoughtfully written comments on his students' work. One of his talents lay in motivating his classes to avoid banal solutions in their assignments. His constant directive was "Never do the obvious." He encouraged the students to see their work as a series of challenges, not problems, and always couched his criticism in humor, never ridicule. One student remembers that in posing an interior design problem involving chinoiserie, Truex advised the class, "Above all, avoid looking like American chop suey."

Another student recalls that Truex was unrelenting in his insistence on the use of appropriate architectural and decorative terms. A long, cushioned seat for two or more people was always a "sofa," never a "couch." He would remind his students that the numerous French variations of the word *couch* could allude to many different things, ranging from "Will you go to bed with me?" to "What a fathead!" He continually pointed out that *drape* was a verb, not a noun. Fabric hung at windows was to be called a drapery or a hanging (he preferred the latter), never a drape.

One of the pleasures Truex derived from being back in New York City was having the chance to see Eleanor McMillen again. In 1925, during his senior year in Paris, she had opened her decorating firm, McMillen, Inc. Offering what she called full-service interior decorating, McMillen had quickly become an important figure in New York. Ever since meeting Truex during his first year in New York, she had been extremely fond of him, and her initial positive impressions had only been strengthened by Odom's praise of the work he did during his senior year in Paris. In her mind, it was a stroke of genius for Parsons to hire the young graduate as a member of the New York faculty. She was a staunch supporter of the school, and she felt that Truex could, in time, become a natural successor to Parsons and Odom. She also knew that if and when that opportunity presented itself, her opinions on the matter would not be taken lightly.

After Parsons and Odom had their annual meeting to "cut up the melon" in December 1926, Parsons announced to Truex that he would be teaching in Paris the next year. Truex would never discover how Odom had achieved this, but he had proven himself to be a man of his word. Parsons also informed Truex that his new teaching responsibilities in Paris would include both advertising art and costume and stage design. The cover that Truex designed for the 1927–1928 school catalog provided an aerial view of New York Harbor, with all of the ocean liners, under steam, shown heading east. Clearly, he was focused on his own Atlantic crossing and his new job at 9 place des Vosges.

In May 1927, Lindbergh made his historic landing in Paris. Even without the fanfare and international acclaim that had greeted the aviator, Truex was thrilled to arrive in the city late that summer. In the fall, Aunt Kee wrote to tell him that J. C. Penney now had five hundred stores, a milestone of growth that also signified continuing financial success for J. S. Truex. In her letter, Aunt Kee assured her nephew that she had passed along to all of the family the good news of his teaching position in Paris. It was an exciting year for both Truexes. But though father and son were definitely aware of each other's success, no words of congratulations or good wishes were exchanged between them.

9 Place des Vosges

When Truex returned to Paris in August 1927, he leased a flat on the Left Bank, at 44 rue du Bac. While his salary was less than he had earned in New York, the devalued French franc allowed him to have two rooms. The drawing room had a fireplace and two windows (which unfortunately gave onto the wall of the building next door); the bedroom also had a fireplace, though no windows. There was no kitchen and, even more inconvenient, no private bath or toilet. But for Truex, the fireplaces, the twelve-foot ceilings, and the nineteenth-century moldings more than compensated for the lack of conveniences and the shortage of light.

Wanting to have his apartment decorated by the time Odom returned from England, in September, Truex used most of his cash reserve to buy furniture. At a *marché aux puces,* he bought two commodes, several small tables, some odd chairs, and a rug. The furniture was all in the style of either Louis-Philippe or Napoleon III, and some pieces were actually of the period. Nothing was of great quality, but everything had a patina. From a neighborhood *brocanteur,* he purchased two painted folding screens that he knew would please his former teacher: one of Odom's many dictums held that screens should be used to break the monotony of the corners of a room. Every object and piece of furniture in Truex's flat was selected according to his mentor's

Truex in the Boboli Gardens, Florence, 1927.

decorating decrees and taste, including the mass arrangements of white flowers that were set out for Odom's first visit.

Soon after Odom returned to Paris, he received a letter from Parsons confiding that he had been quite ill and would undoubtedly have frequent need of Odom's assistance at the New York school. This demand on Odom's time, coupled with his antiques-buying trips, meant that he would be away from the Paris school for much of the year. Odom told Truex that during his absences, he expected him to work closely with his associate Mabel Wilkerson on the daily management of the school. In the same directive, Odom encouraged Truex to make an effort to get to know Grace Fakes, the head of the Department of Interior Architecture and Decoration, who had been one of his teachers during his senior year. Odom was effusive in his praise of Fakes's abilities and fastidious attention to detail. Among her many talents was the ability to produce meticulous watercolor renderings of rooms. Truex soon found that

Place des Vosges, Paris, 1938.

Fakes was the exceptional woman Odom described, but she had a serious fault: she could be a curmudgeon and a tyrant in the classroom. When students submitted their homework assignments to her, they feared the sting of her harsh criticism. Truex's popularity with the students allowed him to come to her rescue, and he became the foil she needed. When her acerbic manner grew unbearable, Truex would use his sense of humor to temper her comments and mend hurt feelings.

Truex and Fakes became more than colleagues: they were allies. He

The entrance (left) *and the fireplace* (right) *of the Grand Gallery, New York School of Fine and Applied Arts, 9 Place des Vosges, Paris, 1938.*

stood as her defense against the students' resentment; she, in turn, was his post-graduate mentor. While Truex had spent countless hours in the safe havens of museums and grand houses, taking exacting measurements and producing drawings of architectural details and *boiserie,* he had never experienced the undaunted curiosity that drove Fakes. She believed that many of the greatest works of art, best examples of architecture, and finest antiques in France had yet to be discovered.

Frequently the two of them went on bicycle trips outside Paris, where Fakes was never shy about gaining entrance to the humblest dwellings or to public buildings if it meant seeing artifacts and architectural details not reproduced in prosaic commentaries on art history and decoration. Under her tutelage, Truex learned that not all of the treasures of the world were to be found in museums or the homes of wealthy people. By encouraging him to look for beauty in modest and unassuming settings, she immeasurably broadened his sense of design. He would incorporate the lessons learned from her into his own teaching, always emphasizing the importance of developing an eye for detail. In his lectures, Truex frequently cited the negative example of those who went to museums and looked all day but never saw anything. He himself maintained a rigorous self-discipline in preparing for his lectures and was meticulous in reviewing the work submitted by his students. Like their peers at the New York school during his first year of teaching, the students in Paris were unwavering in their admiration of and respect for Truex.

Over and above his exceptional teaching skills, Truex also had an appealing, graceful personal manner that was reflected in his ever-correct posture, movements, and gestures. One of his students remembers, "Truex moved like a dancer. He struck a chord of elegance when he entered a room." Men and women alike remarked on his charm and graciousness. With little money to spend on clothes, he became adept at making his minimal wardrobe serve multiple purposes. His pret-a-porter suits, always combined with the perfect

Truex sketching in Aix-en-Provence, 1930.

shirt and a carefully chosen tie, never failed to elicit compliments. His instinct for mixing and matching the few pieces he had was optimized by his natural talent for wearing clothes. He once said, "I was so skinny that jackets hung on my body like a coat displayed on a mannequin."

In the fall of his young protégé's first year on the Paris faculty, Odom arranged for him to be invited to a recital at the home of Princess Edmond de Polignac. Truex's inclusion in Odom's social life would eventually have an unfortunate bearing on their relationship, but in these early days, Odom was delighted to take him along on every occasion. What Odom did not realize was that the princess, like Lady Mendl, often found him conservative to the point of boredom, and that Truex's charm, in stark contrast to Odom's tedium, would win her over.

When they arrived at the party, Odom excused himself from Truex and joined a group of older women, all of whom exuded an aura of old money and privilege. Left to himself, Truex was relieved to be approached by an attractive woman who seemed to exhibit a certain proprietorship over the event. She introduced herself as Violet Trefusis. Aware that he knew no one present, Trefusis made it her business to see that Truex was properly introduced. When the princess entertained, artists and musicians mingled freely with the aristocracy of Paris, a custom not readily endorsed by the elite society. All the people Truex met that evening, or so it seemed to him, were either famous in the worlds of art or music or descended from some prestigious French family or other. Finally, Trefusis introduced Truex to two young Englishmen named Burnet Pavitt, an investment banker, and John Mallet, an attaché at the British Embassy. While neither of the two men displayed any outward signs of wealth, each seemed to possess an innate sense of refinement and quality. Seeing that the young American was comfortable with Pavitt and Mallet, Trefusis moved on, in the company of a handsome woman by the name of Norah Auric. After the two women walked away, Mallet explained to

Truex that Madame Auric was the wife of the composer Georges Auric, one of *les Six,* the group of musicians that included Darius Milhaud, Louis Durey, Arthur Honegger, Francis Poulenc, and Germaine Tailleferre.

Burnet Pavitt on the terrace of André Durst's estate, Paris, 1937.

On first meeting Truex, Pavitt feared that Trefusis had saddled him and Mallet with a "New World novice." Bored by the man, Pavitt admonished him for asking questions about the other guests—who they were and what they did. Realizing that Pavitt wanted to be rid of Truex, Mallet suggested that they all mingle a bit now and meet some other time for lunch. Even after the three men later became the best of friends, Pavitt would always teasingly refer to Truex as "dear Van—New World, you know." That early dismissal, "New World," would be his endearing, and enduring, nickname for Truex.

Before noon the next day, the princess, Trefusis, and Mallet each telephoned Truex. Under the guise of wanting to talk to him in greater detail about his work at the "atelier," as she called the school, the princess invited him to tea. She would later tell Pavitt that her real motive was "to assess just how much I need to teach the charming Mr. Truex."

Trefusis, unabashedly enthusiastic about Truex, invited him to spend a weekend at her country house. She volunteered that Pavitt and Mallet were also coming and suggested that perhaps he could travel with them, being careful to add that if this would not be convenient, other arrangements could be made. Mallet, in his formal British way, asked Truex to lunch with him, Pavitt, and their friend Valentine (known to his friends as Nicholas) Lawford.

John Mallet on the great lawn of Compiègne, France, 1938.

The princess—the former Wineretta Singer, eighteenth child of Isaac Singer, the sewing-machine magnate—was known to be one of the most powerful women in Paris. Along with Comte Etienne de Beaumont and Vicomte and Vicomtesse Charles and Marie de Noailles, she was one of the city's greatest patrons of the arts. But this was only one aspect of her reputation. While her enormous wealth put her above scandal, she was an acknowledged lesbian and the lover of Violet Trefusis. Trefusis, the daughter of Mrs. George Keppel, mistress to King Edward VII, was married to Denys Robert Trefusis. Before her liaison with the princess, Trefusis had had a tempestuous love affair with Vita Sackville-West.

In Trefusis's words, "People quailed before the Princess. Her face was like a landscape with a rugged contour. Her rocky profile seemed to call for ocean spray and seagulls. She had cloudy hair and the small blue eyes of an old salt, that came and went." Trefusis described her lover as a "remarkable, imperturbable, inscrutable, infinitely intimidating, immensely rich woman who was given to making dry, caustic utterances." The princess's house at 57 avenue Henri-Martin was a veritable temple to the arts. Reconstructed in the classic eighteenth-century French style, the public rooms and concert galleries were filled with priceless objects and paintings by Goya, Manet, Monet, Renoir, and Degas. The grand salon, which resembled the Galerie des Glaces at Versailles, regularly served as the setting for concerts and exhibitions of paintings, including the princess's own. Into this world of formidable splendor, at the appointed hour, Truex came for tea and further scrutiny by the princess.

Speaking in French, with no concession to proper pronunciation, the princess immediately announced that while she loved beautiful houses and antiques, she was not at all interested in decorating. She further declared that she adored taste and style in all of the arts, though she singled out music as her real passion. While she was not in the least concerned with fads, she said, she was extremely interested in serious new music. That afternoon, in her magisterial fashion, she began Truex's introduction to great music. Effortlessly, she guided their conversation, which was essentially a brilliant monologue, to the works of Bach, Mozart, Beethoven, and Schubert, and thence to grand opera, often pausing and playing the piano to demonstrate a particular point. While presiding over the most elegant tea Truex had ever been served, the princess spoke about the need for him to shed his American conventions and inhibitions. As their afternoon together came to a close, the princess invited him to call her by her pet name, Tante Winnie, and said that she expected him to come to her musical evenings, where she would introduce him to the most important people in the city—*le tout Paris.* Truex left knowing that he had met his new *maîtresse* and completed the first step in his move into *haute société.*

The weekend visit to Trefusis's house in the country proved to be far more relaxing than Truex's tea with the princess. Thanks to Trefusis, Pavitt and Mallet did invite him to ride with them. Over lunch the previous week, the

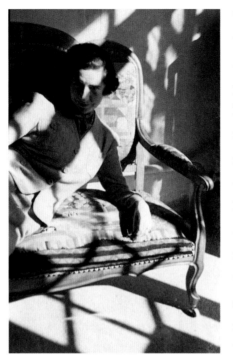

Violet Trefusis.

three had put the awkwardness of their first encounter behind them. Having packed his camera, sketch pads, and best outfits, Truex was delighted by the prospect of seeing Trefusis again. Her house, La Tour, was in St. Loup de Naud, near the medieval town of Provins, some eighty kilometers from Paris. La Tour, a derelict tower, had been bought and renovated for Trefusis as a gift from the princess. While the place had style, many of the rooms were almost inaccessible, and unwary visitors had been known frequently to trip down the narrow and steep stairs. The chimneys had so far to draw that fires in the bedroom grates produced terrible smoke, and the exposed water pipes routinely burst in the winter, causing further discomfort. But in spite of all these inconveniences, La Tour was lavishly furnished with extraordinary art and antiques.

Guests who did not drive were generally told to inquire at the Ritz Hotel in Paris, where the concierge would arrange for a car and driver at Trefusis's expense. People without private incomes were seldom invited to La Tour. Still, having neither a private income nor a car in no way hampered Truex's pleasure on his first or subsequent visits to this place of enchantment, where he enjoyed the luxury of sleeping on an antique canopied bed in a room appointed with chandeliers and Renaissance tapestries.

Norah Auric, the Russian-born artist and engineer whom Truex remembered seeing that first evening at the princess's, was among the myriad guests at La Tour that weekend. Everyone there knew that Auric's husband, Georges, was having his own holiday with the composer Francis Poulenc. Taking separate holidays was part of the Aurics' piquant life-style, an arrangement not unique among fashionable people. Another of Trefusis's guests was Guy de Lesseps, son of the designer of the Suez Canal, who had the private income that was expected of guests at Trefusis's parties. Trefusis was adroit in her ability to mix and match people, and just as her introduction of Truex to Pavitt and Mallet was to result in a lifelong bond among the three men, her inviting him and de Lesseps for the same weekend at La Tour would mark the beginning of another protracted friendship.

Truex's greatest pleasure on his first weekend at La Tour was meeting Princess Elizabeth Chavchavadze. Like the Aurics, the princess and her husband, Prince George Chavchavadze, often traveled separately, and on this particular weekend, Elizabeth Chavchavadze was alone. Truex recognized that there was something exceptional about this woman and made it his business to win her friendship. It was a move he would never regret. Before departing for Paris, Chavchavadze invited him to visit her in Venice after his school closed.

On Sunday afternoon, as Truex, Pavitt, and Mallet drove back to Paris, they were unguarded in sharing humorous stories and gossip garnered over the weekend. In addition to knowing the princess and Trefusis, they all had in common the friendship of Sir Charles and Lady Mendl. Truex was open with the two men about the demands Odom placed on him and how the relationship had kept him from having his own group of friends. The two Englishmen assured Truex that they would be more than happy to introduce him to the world beyond 9 place des Vosges. They further reminded him that this was his first year back in Paris; Pavitt, an inveterate tease, never missed a chance to say, "Don't be so eager, Van."

Just as she had nurtured Truex during his senior year in Paris, Mary Rogers continued to treat him, now that he was back, as a member of her family. She knew that he was beginning to make friends outside of the American community, but the life-style of many of these people ran contrary to her conservative nature. While Rogers's enormous wealth could have brought her into close contact with any group she might have chosen, she was perfectly content in her relationships with Boutet de Monvel, her daughter, Millicent, and her grandson Peter. These three people, plus Truex and her painting, were all she needed. She did enjoy spending time with her American friends when she had the chance, and entertained Janet Weldon, Molly Potter, and Alice Garrett whenever they were in Paris. Like her, these women were amused by some of the goings-on in the city, but they held to their conservative values and customs. Over time, Weldon, Potter, and Garrett would begin to include Truex in their own tight social circles.

Frank Alvah Parsons on the Lido, Venice, 1929.

When Odom returned from New York after the Christmas break, in late January 1927, he brought more bad news about Parsons's health. He told

Truex that he had invited Parsons to spend the spring break with them in Venice; he hoped a complete change and the Adriatic Sea air might do him some good. When Parsons arrived in Paris, he put on a show of being his usual jovial self, but it was obvious that he was very sick. After several days in the city, the three men headed off on their holiday. Parsons amused everyone on the Lido with his flowing robes and fez, and while Odom was not totally comfortable with such high jinks, he worked hard to make the interlude a memorable time for his old mentor. This was the first and the last holiday the three men would spend together.

A few months after returning to New York City, Parsons once again summoned Odom for help. As Odom left Paris, he said that after he gave Parsons whatever assistance he could, he planned to spend the rest of the summer break in England. Before departing, he gave Truex a list of assignments to be completed before the fall term began in September. None of the tasks would require much time or effort, which meant that Truex would be free to travel and enjoy his first real summer off in Europe. He looked forward to visiting the Prince and Princess Chavchavadze in Venice.

Elizabeth Chavchavadze's enormously wealthy father, Henry Ridgeway, had moved from Philadelphia to Paris before the turn of the century. In the manner of Henry James, Ridgeway and his wife had made Europe their home. Their two sons and daughter, all born in France, had been perfectly schooled in the social graces of the haute bourgeoisie and traveled extensively with their parents. After receiving a proper education, Elizabeth had married Comte Jacques de Breteuil. Left a widow by de Breteuil's premature death, she had taken as her second husband a White Russian, Prince George Chavchavadze. Descended from an ancient Georgian family, Chavchavadze was extremely handsome, had an ebullient spirit, and was an accomplished pianist.

As Elizabeth matured, her demeanor reflected an elegance of the sort that comes only from a life of privilege. The exceptional taste she had acquired showed in her manners, in her dress, in the way she managed her household staff—in every minute detail of her life. She treated everyone from royalty to the most humble servant with the utmost respect and consideration. She was intolerant of any racial or ethnic prejudice. Her exuberant spirit was contagious to everyone in her presence. Remembering Elizabeth Chavchavadze,

Hubert de Givenchy would say, "No other woman in that period had her gift for decorating and her sense of style. She was an inspiration." In *The Glass of Fashion,* Cecil Beaton wrote, "She brings such discretion and taste to assembling a room, that the general effect is neither overpowering nor vulgar in its richness (of French and Russian pieces), conveying rather an impression of warmth and cosiness."

The Palazzo Polignac, where the Chavchavadzes lived when in Venice, was, and remains, one of the most magnificent buildings on the Grand Canal. In Elizabeth Chavchavadze's masterful scheme of decorating, sunlight filtered through sheer curtains that barely touched the floor and moved freely in the breeze, creating ever-changing patterns on the floor and walls of every room. In the main salon, huge tufted sofas and lounge chairs covered in Italian silk damasks and velvets were arranged in small seating groups. Here and there, appropriately placed, were eighteenth-century gilded Louis XVI chairs and small canapés upholstered in antique petit point and Italian stripes. The colors gave off a radiance reminiscent of the sparkle of clustered cabochon jewels. Nothing interrupted the sense of perfection. Along the walls of the hallways were long marble-topped consoles, overhung with mirrors or paintings and holding large flower arrangements perfectly scaled for the enormously high ceilings. In each room there were chandeliers and candelabra festooned with prisms of polished rock crystal. The atmosphere changed throughout the day with the shifting sunlight, and even on cloudy, overcast days, the rooms seemed iridescent. At night, the same seductive mood was created by the glow of candles.

George Chavchavadze and Truex's fellow guests spent their days on the Lido. Sitting for hours on the beach and swimming had never interested Truex; he much preferred to spend time alone with Elizabeth at the palazzo. Because he had not been to the manor born, someone would eventually have to show him how to take on the mantle of refinement and make it his own.

That first summer in Venice with Elizabeth Chavchavadze marked the beginning of his transformation. In addition to all she taught him about gracious living, she also instilled in him her intolerance of prejudice. On one occasion, Truex, thinking he was being clever, referred to Jews as "Eskimos," a crude slur he had learned from Lady Mendl. Chavchavadze was quick to tell him that no man she respected would ever use such a word. While open expressions of anti-Semitism were common, even de rigueur, in some circles, she would not allow them in her presence.

Still exhilarated by his time at the Palazzo Polignac, Truex returned to Paris in early September to begin his second year of teaching. That fall, Janet Flanner noted in an installment of her "Letter from Paris" that November 18, 1927, marked the fifth anniversary of the death of Proust. The fact that Flanner thought it important enough to write about in *The New Yorker* raises the question, were people refusing to let go and holding tight to things past because they could not find any real meaning in everything new that was happening? Whatever conclusions may be drawn, the dawn of 1928 would bring more of the same wild abandon that had followed World War I. Innovations in art, music, theater, and literature seemed to be endless. Women continued dieting to look boyishly thin. The French, while suspicious of most things "American," loved cocktails and jazz. Costume balls and extravagant parties were the order of the day and the night. There was no indication that a storm was brewing in the American stock market. The indulgent life showed no signs of slowing down. Surely no one thought it would ever end.

Dramatic Changes and Promotion

When the fall semester of 1928 opened—Truex's second year on the faculty at the Paris school—his boyish good looks were being supplanted by a mature handsomeness. His blond hair, blue eyes, firm jaw, and patrician features continued to be admired wherever he went. While some of his friends teased him about his monastic austerity, they all respected his fierce regimen of diet and discipline; with one important exception, his remarkable demeanor elicited unanimous approval. Unfortunately, that fall, Odom began finding fault with him. As Truex became more popular with *le tout Paris*—and especially with certain women, such as Lady Mendl and the Princess de Polignac, whom Odom considered "his" friends— a rift developed between the two men. Odom's place at the exclusive parties given by wealthy and socially prominent people was more and more frequently occupied by the alluring young man on his faculty. Without even realizing it, Truex had upstaged his master.

But whatever Odom may have come to think of him, Truex was the product of his tutelage. When Truex first arrived in New York, in 1923, he had the advantage of total innocence and no bad training that needed to be expunged. Parsons had subsequently opened his eyes to the very best of everything in Manhattan. Then, during Truex's senior year in Paris, Odom had made sure that he was never exposed to anything pedestrian. Now, having

Truex with Mrs. Henry Hazen Hyde, Paris, 1935.

nurtured the young man's sagacious nature and exposed him to the brightest lights of Paris, Odom was annoyed by his popularity. As Truex received more and more attention, he failed to sense Odom's growing resentment. In an attempt to conceal his jealousy and maintain the loyalty of his young rival, Odom announced to the faculty that Truex would be the new head of the Department of Costume and Stage Design. While Odom's peace offering was no doubt sincere, it ultimately would do little to assuage his own burgeoning paranoia.

As the list of privileged people in Truex's address book expanded, he continued to spend time with Pavitt and Mallet. Out of everyone he had met in Paris, he felt most at ease with his two English friends. Like him, they didn't have much money, which made life simpler when they were together. If money was ever a real problem for Truex, it did not remain so for long. Whenever he was with Mary Rogers, she never failed to tuck an envelope of bills into his pocket, saying that she wanted to be sure he was comfortable. Aunt Kee continued to send him money on his birthday and at Christmas, and with the passage of time, her checks had gotten larger. With these gifts and the salary increase that accompanied his new faculty position, Truex's financial situation was such that he was able to think about getting an apartment with a private bath and toilet; he finally concluded, however, that he would be wiser to start building a savings account. His vivid recollections of having nothing and going without always kept him from doing anything impetuous.

Despite the tensions between him and Odom, the end of the spring term of the 1928–1929 school year marked another period of accomplishment in Truex's teaching career. When school opened in the fall of 1929, the two men both worked hard to avoid conflicts, but there were moments—and often prolonged periods—of strain between them. On the surface, it appeared that this would be a year of unbounded success for the school. Enrollment was at a record high, and projected plans for study and travel in Italy and England were more extensive than ever before. With the further devaluation of the French franc, combined with the American vision of unending prosperity, Truex decided that the time had come for him to move to a more comfortable flat, and he found what he wanted at 192 rue de l'Université. His move was barely completed, and school had been open for only a few weeks, when the bubble burst. On Tuesday, October 24, Wall Street stock prices plummeted, and the Great Depression began.

At both branches of the New York School of Fine and Applied Arts, in New York and Paris, student fees were always prepaid, so the financial disaster brought few immediate changes. Nonetheless, Frank Parsons was devastated. There was every reason for him to worry: his school had no support other than student fees and tuition, and most of the students were young women from wealthy families that would probably be ruined by the crash. The economic situation might even mean the end for the school. Odom, ever conscious of Parsons's precarious health and anxiety, sailed in early November 1929 for New York. His ship was filled with expatriate Americans who felt that in the current financial crisis they would be better off at home, and wanted to make the trip while they could still afford passage.

In Paris, Truex's close friends were among the fortunate few who had seen the crash coming and withdrawn their money from the stock market. Many of them were now richer than they had been before. Most Americans, however, were not so lucky—and this certainly included Truex's parents. Two years before, in 1927, his father had retired at the age of fifty-seven from the J. C. Penney Company. Having made a great deal of money from his stock options in the company, J. S. Truex was then a very rich man. In 1928, skeptical about the future of Penney's, he had sold all his stock in the corporation, reinvested the profits in other companies, and bought a large estate in Pacific Palisades, California. In the crash of 1929, J.S. lost everything, including his house. He and Estel were forced to move to a ranch in rural Escondido. Aunt

Kee and Uncle Bert Nicol, unlike Truex's parents, had held on to their J. C. Penney stock and would eventually become enormously rich.

As the financial crisis worsened, Parsons's health continued to decline. On May 26, 1930, at age sixty-two, Frank Alvah Parsons died. Since launching the New York School of Fine and Applied Arts in 1907, he had earned a reputation for maintaining the highest scholastic standards. In the twenty-three years he presided over the school, he received numerous academic honors and citations, including the Chevalier de la Légion d'Honneur. He had the unique distinction of being the first educator to offer courses in interior design.

Long before his death, Parsons had made the necessary legal arrangements for Odom immediately to succeed him and have full control of the school. At forty-six, William Odom became president and director of the

Joseph B. Platt, Little Compton, Rhode Island, 1944.

New York and Paris schools. The added responsibility made it essential that he have a qualified assistant. Truex would have been a natural choice, but Odom, still not over his petty jealousy, said that at just twenty-six, he was too young and lacked the necessary experience to head up the Paris atelier.

Desperately needing help, Odom cajoled Joseph B. Platt, a successful New York designer and graduate of the school, into accepting the job as his director in Paris. Nine years older than

Truex, Platt was extremely talented, driven to work hard, and possessed of an inexhaustible ambition to gain professional recognition. Odom did not mince words in declaring that these were valuable qualities that Truex lacked. He was now openly critical of his former protégé and what he considered to be his indulgent behavior. Platt's wife, June, added to her husband's attractiveness; she was charming and had always been kind to Odom when he was in New York City. The care and concern that the young couple had shown for Parsons during the last year of his life had also won favor with Odom. Unquestionably, Platt was one of the school's most brilliant graduates. Already a successful illustrator when he enrolled, he had earned a double major in Advertising Design and Interior Design and graduated three years later with highest honors. Platt wanted no part of the social limelight unless it could promote his career. Immediately after his graduation, he had been hired as an art director by a leading New York design firm and had also begun to teach part-time at the school. Before he died, Parsons had named Platt the school's director of professional policy, which meant that he was to instruct the students in the business principles of both advertising and interior design.

With reluctance, in the fall of 1930, Joseph and June Platt moved to Paris. They referred to themselves as "the poor Gerald and Sara Murphy," in a nod to the rich American couple now credited with inventing the French Riviera. When they arrived, Truex swallowed his hurt pride and became their guide to the city, and the three of them grew to be close friends. From the beginning, Platt thought Truex would have been perfect for the Paris job, but on observing the young man's social life, he quickly realized why Odom had refused to give him the position. He did not hesitate to speak frankly with Truex about his priorities, telling him that he could have a brilliant future at the school if only he would reconcile his differences with Odom. Knowing that Platt's advice was being offered on a purely professional basis, Truex listened and took his suggestions to heart. Never having wanted the job in the first place, Platt used every opportunity with Odom to trumpet Truex's abilities and promote him for the position.

With his professional commitments back in New York, Platt hated living in Paris. Once he was there, he found that the responsibilities of running the school were much too demanding and encroached on the time he needed for his design commissions. In the spring of 1931, therefore, after a single academic year in Paris, he resigned and returned to Manhattan. He continued to work hard to persuade Odom that Truex should be made the assistant director in charge of the Paris atelier. Overworked and overwhelmed by the task of managing both schools, Odom knew he had to do *something,* so on Platt's advice, in September 1931, he appointed Truex to be his assistant director in Paris. Two years later, after further endorsement from Platt and support from Eleanor Brown and Elsie Mendl, Odom made him the head of the Paris school and associate director of the New York School of Fine and Applied Arts. When Truex turned thirty, in March 1934, Mary Rogers, her daughter, Millicent, and Aunt Kee each sent him a large check to mark the occasion and celebrate his promotion. Aunt Kee took great pride in her nephew's accomplishments: whenever he sent her a magazine article or newspaper clipping about his work, she would circulate the news within the family, endearingly referring to him as "our Van."

Another person who began adding to Truex's financial well-being around this time was Mrs. Harrison (Mona) Williams, whose husband's fortune, in pre-Depression dollars, was estimated at $700 million. Truex's introduction to this remarkable woman came when Elsa Schiaparelli invited him to escort her to a party that Mrs. Williams was giving at her apartment in the famous Hôtel Lambert. Even though he had often heard Schiaparelli speak of the exotic Mona Williams, Truex was overwhelmed by her ravishing beauty. Describing Williams, Cecil Beaton wrote, "Her complexion radiates the immaculate perfection of health, a perfection which [is] further emphasized by the brilliance of her aquamarine eyes, the sheen of her skin, her strong and energetic hands, and the live muscular body that possesses the élan of a released spring." In time, Mona Williams would become one of Truex's closest friends.

After he was put in charge in Paris, Truex, wherever he was or whatever he was doing, always worked to promote the school. Under his leadership, the list of the school's patrons soon included every important person in the French decorative arts. The directors of Malmaison, Versailles et les Trianons, Fontainebleau, the Palais de Compiègne, the Musée du Louvre, the Musée des Arts Décoratifs, and the Musée Carnavalet, as well as the director general of the École des Beaux-Arts, were all affiliated with the school, as

were prominent Americans such as Mrs. Edith Wharton, Mrs. William K. Vanderbilt, the Honorable Mrs. Reginald Fellowes, Lady Mendl, Mr. Ogden Codman, Jr., Mr. Walter Gay, and the Honorable Jesse Straus, the United States ambassador to France. While Odom had initiated contact with many of these people, it was Truex who secured their loyalty to the school.

During Truex's tenure, the Princess de Polignac and Mrs. John Garrett were but two of the many wealthy

Truex on the Piazza della Signoria, Florence, 1927.

people who were persuaded to help the school with generous contributions. After the designer Louis Süe completed his extensive refurbishing and decorating of Daisy Fellowes's eighteenth-century house in Neuilly-sur-Seine, he encouraged his client to host a fund-raising event for Truex's institution. Fellowes had met Truex through her aunt, the Princess de Polignac, and was only too happy to oblige. In the spectacular main salon of her house, originally designed for the Duc d'Artois, brother of Louis XIV, she entertained Truex and potential supporters of the school. Boosted by such solid financial support, Truex played his trump card and invited the interior decorators Stephane Boudin, Jean-Michel Frank, and Serge Roche, along with the graphic artist Cassandre (Adolph-Jean-Marie Mouron), to join the faculty. These most elite designers in France all accepted his invitation.

Ever aware of his responsibilities, Truex viewed his place in the world of money and privilege as a means to further the success of the school. In his mind, knowing the right people and being in the right places provided the venues he needed for fund-raising. Extensive though his social obligations were, the American Protestant work ethic, so deeply instilled in him from his youth, never allowed him to dismiss even the smallest detail of his professional responsibilities. Someone without his strength of character, placed in the same situation, might easily have turned into a hapless dilettante, but not Truex: he managed the affairs of the school with great skill and developed into an exceptional teacher and administrator. His greatest satisfaction lay in seeing students succeed in their work, and he was always deeply concerned about the welfare of every one of them. As word of his success in Paris crossed the Atlantic, his place of favor with Odom was restored. Odom often spoke with Eleanor Brown about the exemplary job Truex was doing; she was not at all surprised.

Each year, when Truex returned to New York City for the show of the Paris students' work, he was welcomed as Odom's golden boy. Under Truex's direction, the Paris atelier became much more than just a branch of the New York school: it was a European institution. No other school in England or on the continent offered the kind of education that was advanced in the programs at 9 place des Vosges. According to Stanley Barrows, the most revered member of the New York school's faculty, "Odom and Truex taught the Europeans how to decorate. They had all the raw ingredients, the best art, the best architecture, the best furniture and design, but they didn't know how to put it together. It was all in museums or vast manor houses and châteaux."

In an interview recorded for the Archives of American Art Oral History Project at the National Gallery of Art in 1971, Truex explained, "What we were teaching in Paris was absolutely unique. The French loved us and our program. There was a fascination with anything American. In the thirties they still thought of the United States as the Promised Land. All of the major figures in the French decorative arts and the director of every museum did everything possible to support the Paris school, the faculty and students, and our method of teaching." The Paris program attracted not only young students but also a large number of mature men and women from England and the continent who wanted to learn the skills and techniques of interior decorating. Under Truex's guidance, the school continued to require rigorous study in art history, period design, and academic drawing, as well as total immersion in the neoclassical tradition. The intellectual elite of the art world remained critical of the school's curriculum, viewing it as decidedly old-fashioned and irrelevant to modern design, but such criticism did not move Truex and Odom. Neither man wavered in his support of Parsons's founding principles.

The Director

hen Truex began his tenure as director of the Paris school, in 1934, the Great Depression continued to worsen in the United States. That same year, Franklin Roosevelt, then in his first term as president, assured the nation that "the only thing we have to fear is fear itself." Fifteen million Americans were unemployed, and wages had dropped 50 percent over the previous five years. In the Northeast, unskilled and industrial workers struggled to survive. In the South, the black population was terrorized by an outbreak of lynchings: over 70 percent of the black population still lived south of the Mason-Dixon Line, and in 1933, forty-two blacks had been killed by lynch mobs. By 1936, 38 percent of the country's families would be living below the poverty line, with annual incomes of less than one thousand dollars.

Those Americans who had cashed in their stocks before the crash lived comfortably above the fray. Reporting on life among the rich in New York City in 1932, Cecil Beaton wrote in *Vogue:*

> *The poverty is only comparative. A hey-hey spirit prevails, and there are many signs of festivity. . . . Mrs. Fair Vanderbilt has never been busier entertaining. There are enough small parties, with cold turkey and champagne, to keep any boy out late every night of the week. There has*

Truex's apartment, Paris, 1938.

been no dimming of the lights on Broadway. . . . Nothing is skimped on, simple or economical about the new River Club. Here [in New York] it is impossible to believe that we live in hard times. . . . Certainly, the most amazing phenomenon of the present poverty-stricken, panic-stricken season is the new Waldorf–Astoria Hotel. It is the largest hotel that has been built since the world began.

In the Paris community of wealthy people from South America and the United States, the devastating economic crisis in America made little impact. These same people had less interest in Europe's shifting political arena. While there was also a financial depression in Paris, the rich—French and expatriate alike—amused themselves in fancy-dress parties. "Parties, Parties, Parties . . . there were even parties to raise money for the unemployed, not that they [the unemployed] were invited," reported *Vogue*. The article went on to say, "Long, stuffy, boring, and many course dinners regimented by social decorum were things of the past." The international set even indulged themselves in a craze for nursery games and played musical chairs, blindman's buff, and stick the pig.

Many of the most extravagant parties were orchestrated by Elsa Maxwell. Obsessed with the world of celebrities, Maxwell was a social impresario, best remembered today as the inventor of public relations and the person who revived the Lido. She was paid between sixteen thousand and sixty thousand dollars to make other people's parties sparkle. Her biggest job was for the Greek government, which hired her to promote tourism in Greece. Her parties set a standard with their unsurpassed gaiety and, often, vulgarity. Despite Maxwell's outrageous behavior, or perhaps because of it, Cole Porter was one of her closest friends; he dubbed her the "Queen of Paris." Her best-known event was a notorious scavenger hunt in which guests had to scour

Paris for a series of ridiculous items, including a live swan from the Bois de
Boulogne, a hat belonging to Daisy Fellowes, a live duchess, the cleverest man
in the city, and a slipper worn by Jeanne Bourgeois, alias Mistinguett, the celebrated French chanteuse and star of the Casino de Paris. On the night of the
infamous hunt, Mistinguett's frightened maid didn't stand a chance when the
rummaging revelers invaded the star's dressing room. Returning to find all of
her shoes gone, the enraged entertainer vented her wrath on the terrorized
servant, declaring the scavenger hunters a band of barbarians. The following
morning, all was forgiven when the shoes were returned, tied to massive flow-
ering plants and bunches of orchids.

The biggest sensations during these years, however, were costume balls
of ravishing elegance, attended by the *gens du monde* and the most celebrated
of Parisian painters, poets, writers, and artists. Prince Jean-Louis de Faucigny-
Lucinge and his wife, Baba, Comte and Comtesse Etienne de Beaumont, and
Vicomte and Vicomtesse de Noailles were among the most assiduous party
givers. These elaborate affairs, which ideally were held outdoors, usually began
at ten in the evening or later and went on until after dawn; totally and completely frivolous, they celebrated the ephemeral and gave revelers a chance to
enjoy themselves as children might. Truex generally retired early, but he disciplined himself to take an afternoon nap and at least make an appearance at
such events, seeing the connections he made socially as a necessary part of his
job. It was a fair exchange: Lady Mendl, one of the prime financial supporters
of the school, could not imagine having a party, even a small luncheon, without Truex.

While Truex had been introduced to Lady Mendl (then Elsie de Wolfe)
by Frank Parsons during his first year in New York, and had later visited her in
Paris with Odom, his relationship with her had blossomed after a chance encounter in Antibes, at the Grand Hôtel du Cap. Eden Roc, as the hotel was

known, was then a millionaires' paradise and served as F. Scott Fitzgerald's inspiration for the fictional Hotel des Etrangers in *Tender Is the Night*. When Truex ran into her at Eden Roc, de Wolfe was the wife of Sir Charles Mendl; both her unacclaimed acting career and her "Boston marriage" to Elizabeth Marbury, a noted New York theatrical agent, were in her past. Her international reputation as an interior decorator was well established, and making money, entertaining, and being entertained had become Lady Mendl's favorite pastimes. At Eden Roc, she insisted that Truex begin visiting her more frequently in Versailles and invited him to call her Elsie. While Truex would never forget that Mary Rogers was his first obligation, Lady Mendl's Paris apartment and Villa Trianon, her house in Versailles, would soon become his regular haunts.

In addition to convincing Truex that beige was the only color that mattered, Lady Mendl furthered his relationship with Elsa Schiaparelli. Since her acting days, Mendl had always loved fashion and celebrated designers. She took full credit for Mainbocher's success, boasting that her wearing an outfit or a gown added luster to the reputation of its designer. Mainbocher, Valentina (along with her husband, George Schlee), and Schiaparelli were all frequent visitors at Villa Trianon. Each season, when the new collections were shown in Paris, Lady Mendl gave a fete that was attended by every designer of note, including the current star of American fashion, Charles James.

Whenever Kitty Miller, daughter of the American financier Jules Bache, and her husband, Gilbert, the English and American theatrical producer, were in Paris, Lady Mendl always invited them to Villa Trianon. It was there that Truex first met the couple. Kitty Miller was extremely rich, demanding, and often quite mean-spirited, but when the mood struck her, she could be both kind and generous. When she met Truex, she was concerned, like Mona Williams and Mary Rogers before her, that he had to struggle on what she called "a poor teacher's salary"; soon she, too, began making discreet additions to his accounts.

At Lady Mendl's parties, her guests could be sure of three things. First, there would be very little food; it was well known that if you wanted to get something to eat, you had to arrive early. Second, the hostess would be wearing white gloves. Third, the guests would include a coterie of handsome, and entertaining, young men. Truex, Pavitt, and Mallet, along with the

Sergio Pizzoni, 1935.

American playboy Howard Sturges; Derek Hill, the English painter; Fulco di Verdura, the widely touted young jewelry designer; and Niki de Gunzburg, a writer for *Town and Country* and *Vogue,* were always on her invitation list. Lady Mendl's criteria for the men she invited to her parties were good looks, good manners, and brilliant conversation. She didn't bother listening to anything that didn't have a modicum of wit. Even more, she loved wicked anecdotes and gossip.

When Truex first met Pavitt and Mallet, in 1926, they had already been living together for years. Besides enjoying their company, Truex admired and respected the way they conducted their lives. They never tried to conceal their relationship, but they lived beyond reproach. Whereas other people, such as the Princess de Polignac and Violet Trefusis, were protected from scandal by their vast wealth, it was Pavitt and Mallet's gentlemanly behavior and perfect decorum that shielded them from any criticism. Their good looks and charm made them the favored guests of every celebrated Parisian hostess. Through them, Truex was introduced to the fashion photographer André Durst. Then in his prime at *Vogue,* Durst had just completed work on his new country house, Chez André, on the edge of Montfontaine. It was there that Truex met Oliver Messel, the English set designer; Georges Geoffroy, a fashion illustrator who would later become a much-celebrated interior decorator in Paris; and the photographers George Hoyningen-Huene and Horst P. Horst. Jean Schlumberger, Cecil Beaton, and Valentine (Nicholas) Lawford, whom Truex had previously met through Schiaparelli, also routinely participated in the revelry at Chez André.

In 1934, at a party given by Coco Chanel, Truex met a young Italian named Sergio Pizzoni, who had recently moved to Paris to improve his skills in French and English. When Pizzoni realized that Truex was fluent in both languages, he proposed that they begin meeting on a regular basis. Goaded by Pavitt and Mallet's admonitions to be less reserved, Truex agreed to Pizzoni's

William Odom and Sergio Pizzoni, 1938.

proposal. Their chance encounter marked the beginning of a liaison that would last for the next five years.

Whenever the two men met, at first for meals or walks in the Tuileries Gardens, Pizzoni's youthful enthusiasm was countered by Truex's cautious nature. As they became closer, Truex worried that the relationship might pose a problem with his conservative American friends. He was certain that Mary Rogers, for one, would have no interest in his new friend. While she adored Truex, Rogers had never asked any questions about his personal life. He was fully aware that it would be unacceptable for him ever to bring along a male companion when he visited her. He did, however, have one friend, Grace Bingham, who he was sure would welcome Pizzoni.

Truex had first met Grace Bingham on the Lido. A wealthy American who owned an apartment in Paris and a villa in Cannes, she lived a life free of conventions, never having had any use for what she called "stuffy society people and their overbearing rules." Bingham followed no rules. The best example of her free spirit was her devotion to Elsa Maxwell. Most people, including those who paid for her services, deemed Maxwell was a terrible, foul-mouthed woman who was to be feared and, at all costs, not to be crossed. But Bingham, like Cole Porter, found Maxwell's company to be enormous fun, and because they were great friends, she never had to pay her to brighten up a party.

While the fashionable women on the Riviera were starving themselves to be thin and have figures like little boys, Bingham took genuine delight in being curvaceous. Her idea of having nothing to do was attending a party where the hostess served little bits of food that she called lunch. Once, when Bingham was in Paris, Truex took her along with him to Villa Trianon. Pavitt wasted no time in telling him that he had committed a terrible faux pas, pointing out that Bingham was too loud (which was true) and that glances of disapproval were being exchanged not only by the ladies present, but by some of the men, too. Bingham couldn't have cared less. She laughed too loud, she knew it, and she meant to do it. She was also a salacious flirt. When Truex asked if he could bring Pizzoni to one of her parties, Bingham was delighted.

Before they arrived, Truex advised Pizzoni not to expect to meet any intellectuals or hear any erudite conversation. His prediction proved right. As usual, Bingham was surrounded by friends who had no patience with bourgeois society. Maxwell, more outrageous than ever, was there, as were Dorothy and Bill Paley and Bingham's new boyfriend, a dashingly handsome American named Geoffrey Gates. As Truex had anticipated, Bingham adored his new friend. Pizzoni, for his part, was quite adept at attending social functions with a male companion; he knew when it was appropriate for him to be close by his friend's side and when it was proper to mingle with the other guests. Truex, once again the novice, followed Pizzoni's lead.

The product of an upbringing no less privileged than Elizabeth Chavchavadze's, Pizzoni was unquestionably the most elegant man Truex had ever met. While his private income absolved him of any need to work, Pizzoni was extremely disciplined in his study of languages, literature, and art history. He was confident that when the time came for him to decide on a career, the best course would become apparent. For the years he was with Truex, Pizzoni was perfectly happy to immerse himself in the pursuit of French culture and the social life of Paris.

In the spring of 1934, as the Easter holidays approached, Pizzoni invited Truex to his family's estate, the Villa Valsanzibio, near Padua. Known as the Jewel of the Veneto, surrounded by orchards and vineyards, the fourteenth-century villa was magnificently sited on a hillside. Terraced formal gardens, intended to represent man's progression to perfection, led from the entrance gates to the villa's front steps. Every room within was exquisitely furnished with Re-

Truex snapshots of a weekend at Grace Bingham's villa, La Corne d'Or, 1934. Clockwise from top: The villa on the Riviera; Geoffrey Gates; Elsa Maxwell swimming; Grace Bingham.

Villa Valsanzibio, the family estate of Sergio Pizzoni, near Padua, Italy, 1935.

naissance and eighteenth-century antiques and paintings. The Villa Valsanzibio was the most impressive private home Truex had ever visited. In addition to the laborers in the vineyards and orchards, the Pizzoni family employed thirty gardeners and a household staff of more than twenty uniformed servants.

From the moment of Truex's arrival until his last farewell, Pizzoni's mother and father showed him the same respect and care they lavished on Sergio and their younger son, Fabio. Their hospitality and nurture were beyond anything he had ever experienced. Every year until Truex left France, in 1939, he and Pizzoni would spend at least two weeks each spring and summer at the villa, where the warm welcome and graciousness of the Pizzoni family always awaited them. Recalling those visits, Fabio Pizzoni says, "My parents were devoted to Van. My mother was especially fond of him. I only remember that he and my brother were both very handsome and I looked up to them as special people. When mother died and Sergio inherited the villa, he had the family sitting room decorated in beige. I am sure this was because of Van. He had a significant influence on all of us. When he came back to the villa after the war, my wife had died; I always regretted that she did not know him. Van Day Truex was a remarkable man."

Each year of Truex's tenure as director of the Paris school, from 1933 until 1939, the political situation in Europe worsened. Hitler began his dictatorship of Nazi Germany in 1933, and a year later, after von Hindenburg died, garnered the votes he needed to take over the presidency of Germany. That same year, he assumed the title of Führer. In 1935, he denounced the Versailles Treaty, which demanded Germany's disarmament, and organized the German Luftwaffe. In 1937, Hitler's new German air forces and Spanish rebels destroyed the town of Guernica, in Spain. To promote his "master plan," Hitler offered financial incentives for Germans to marry Germans and gave cash awards for each child produced. Under his rule, the Nuremberg Laws forbade intermarriage between Aryans and Jews; even "mixed" intercourse was a capital offense. German Jews were evicted from trade and industry, barred from city parks, entertainment, resorts, and public institutions, and forced to wear a yellow six-pointed Star of David. By 1938, Austrian Jews were denied civil rights and deprived of any means of earning a living.

The rise of Mussolini in Italy and that of Stalin in Russia only enhanced the sense of ominousness. By 1936, the Great Purge had begun in the Soviet Union; within two years, more than eight million would die as a result of Stalin's ruthlessness and paranoia. Economic woes and persistent memories of the Great War enforced a spirit of isolationism in the United States, even as American corporations made enormous investments in Germany, lending financial support to Hitler's new Deutschland.

Truex with Vicomtesse Marie-Laure de Noailles, at the Villa Noailles, in the heights of Hyères, near Nice, 1937.

In February 1934, France faced the possibility of civil war, and in 1936, riots raged in Paris. The xenophobia and economic strife that plagued the nation were little altered by the two international exhibitions that were staged during this decade to promote French progress. The 1931 Exposition Coloniale prompted sharp criticism from both the Left and the Right. While the 1937 Exposition Internationale des Arts et Techniques de la Vie drew bigger crowds than the 1925 Exposition des Arts Décoratifs, it also brought the presence of Germany and Russia and their enormous pavilions to Paris. When the 1937 exposition opened, the great spirit of creativity that had been nurtured in Paris after the Great War was all but dead. By then the establishment no longer wanted anything to do with experimental art. Most Frenchmen preferred to live in a fantasy world that evoked the past glories of France. Most people with money wanted to have a good time and not think about the possibility of another war.

When the rich became even slightly bored, they took to heart Cole Porter's dictum "There's No Cure Like Travel," and travel they did. If good times were not to be had in Paris, there was always Vienna, Venice, Ravenna, Siena, Florence, or Rome. Wherever the elite went, Truex went with them. His social life and life in the atelier at 9 place des Vosges continued to flourish. Expatriate Americans for the most part believed that if there was going to be a war, the United States would not be involved—and there, their concern ended. The prevailing mood was summed up in a conversation overheard at one of Lady Mendl's Sunday lunches, where someone asked if anyone at the table had ever known a Czechoslovakian. One man admitted that his valet was of that nationality but said he was hardly worth fighting for.

While expatriate Americans lived the high life in Paris and Venice, most people in the United States were struggling just to survive. President Roosevelt continued to do everything in his power to bring hope to the American people, but his Civilian Conservation Corps, Works Progress Administration, Social Security Act, and other programs of economic relief all met with bitter opposition from the established rich. Along with devastating dust storms and drought in the Midwest, in 1934 the United States faced the alarming possibility of the first general strike in the nation's history. The downward economic spiral that had begun in 1929 seemed to know no end. In 1937, Aunt Kee wrote to Truex that his parents had suffered further financial losses. Both in poor health, they could no longer afford to keep their ranch in Escondido and had been forced to move to a small rented bungalow in La Jolla.

When Americans could scrape together the price of admission in these years, going to the movies became their favored escape from the crisis. The fantasy of motion pictures provided some emotional relief. Fred Astaire and Ginger Rogers danced their way into the hearts of millions in *Flying Down to*

Rio, Top Hat, Swing Time, and *Shall We Dance?* America found hope in *Gone With the Wind* and a sense of abandon in *Gold Diggers of 1935, Snow White and the Seven Dwarfs,* and *Fantasia.* And everyone fell in love with a little girl named Shirley Temple singing "The Good Ship *Lollipop.*"

As the financial depression grew worse, prohibition ended, Howard Johnson offered twenty-eight flavors of ice cream, Campbell canned chicken soup, Hormel produced Spam, Margaret Rutledge baked Pepperidge Farm bread, DuPont made nylon for stockings, and Americans drank pineapple juice for the first time and shopped at the new Walgreen's Drugstores. During these same years, a red-nosed reindeer named Rudolph made first his appearance in a children's Christmas booklet given away by Montgomery Ward. Lincoln Kirstein founded the New York City Ballet and brought George Balanchine from Europe to be its choreographer; George Gershwin wrote *Porgy and Bess;* and, because she was black, Marian Anderson was denied permission by the Daughters of the American Revolution to sing in Constitution Hall.

Cole Porter captured the spirit of the nation in his hit show *Anything Goes.* In the summer of 1939, New York opened a World's Fair. After Hitler invaded Poland that September, England and France declared war on Germany. Americans waited anxiously to "read all about it" in the new weekly magazines *Life, Newsweek,* and *Look.* Bringing the reality of the war closer to home, after the German air raids on England in 1940, Edward R. Murrow went on the radio each night and announced gravely, "This is London . . . ," before proceeding to report the horrors of the blitz. A frightened British people sang, and believed, "There'll Always Be an England." Americans, trying to forget their own economic woes and confident that they would be spared this conflict, sang "Miss Otis Regrets," "Smoke Gets in Your Eyes," and "It's Only Make-Believe."

It was during these years of turbulence that Truex was finally able to shed the rigid aesthetic of William Odom and begin developing a style of his own. While he did not completely abandon his commitment to eighteenth-century French design, he began to view the work of the period, and particularly the Louis XVI manner, in a new light. This shift began quite by chance, when he accompanied Schiaparelli to Jean-Michel Frank's atelier to see the designs for her new salon. After this meeting, their second encounter, Truex and Frank began to develop a bond. Through his association with the French designer, Truex would start to see, and to paint, in a dramatically new way.

The Purge

*I*f Jean-Michel Frank helped Truex fine-tune his definitive style, there can be no doubt, however, that it was William Odom who was responsible for the early development of his taste. It must also be acknowledged that Truex was heavily influenced by Lady Mendl. Essentially, Odom provided him with a background in art history and antiques but gave him little practical knowledge. While Odom's impeccable taste made him a successful purveyor of antiques to wealthy clients and prominent American decorators, he had no interest in the mechanics of implementing decorating concepts. It was Lady Mendl who taught Truex about the practical aspects of interior decorating. She was completely committed to the *business* of the profession. As much as she loved beautiful things, she loved making money even more. Reflecting on her shrewd business practices in his later years, Truex would jokingly refer to Lady Mendl as "a gangster."

While much of Truex's time at Villa Trianon was spent socializing with ambassadors, wealthy Americans, and women and men of fashion, he and Lady Mendl always reserved ample private time to talk about the business of interior decorating. In these conversations, she frequently verged on tedium, repeating over and over her credo "Simplicity, suitability, and proportion." Truex was often tempted to ask her if she hadn't borrowed this from Edith Wharton's decree "Simplicity, suitability, and authenticity," but he knew bet-

Truex wash painting, Dubrovnik, Yugoslavia, from the estate of Mrs. Ottavio Prochet, private collection.

ter. Mrs. Wharton was never discussed in Lady Mendl's presence. Mendl was always painfully aware that despite all her success and acclaim, she would never be accepted into Wharton's lofty world. (Whenever Odom was well out of earshot of Lady Mendl and heard her recite her constant refrain "Simplicity, suitability, and proportion," he would always remind anyone who was listening that it was Louis XIV who had first proclaimed "Order, regularity, and appropriateness." But as far as Lady Mendl was concerned, the mandate was a de Wolfe original!)

The spectacularly gifted Jean-Michel Frank had his own credo: "Proportion, space, form, and matter." No sudden burst of genius, Frank's unique ability had instead evolved over years of exposure to art, antiques, and exceptionally talented people. Like many of the early and most successful decorators, he had no formal training. While he was blessed with many mentors, Frank was most strongly influenced by one extraordinary woman who helped mold and distill his taste and ideas.

Frank had been born in Paris in 1895. His two older brothers had been killed in World War I, and soon after that tragic loss, his father had committed suicide. Four years later, his mother died in an asylum. Fortunately, Frank inherited enough money to pursue his love of the arts and of travel. While on a trip to Venice, he befriended Sergei Diaghilev and his coterie of artists, dancers, and musicians. This encounter would have a significant influence on the development of Frank's career, but even more important would be his association with Madame Eugenia Errazuriz. She played much the same role in Frank's life that Elizabeth Chavchavadze later would fill in Truex's.

Madame Errazuriz, a wealthy South American, had arrived in Europe in the 1880s and immediately become a commanding social figure. Cecil Beaton would describe her remarkable taste as "a unique blend of aristocratic style and peasant simplicity. Everything she did—from the clothes she wore, the flowers she arranged, the food she served, to the rooms she decorated—

was elegant." Her motto was "Throw out, and keep throwing out! When you've finished, throw out some more. Elegance means simplicity."

Like everyone who met her, Frank was fascinated by Madame Errazuriz, mesmerized by her taste and charm. Her influence on Frank, and Chavchavadze's on Truex, beg the tantalizing question, Are women better decorators than men? The superiority of women's decorating abilities was promoted in 1879 by Jakob von Faulke, who wrote, "Taste in women may be natural to their sex. A woman is mistress of the house which she orders like a queen." Lady Mendl confirmed Faulke's opinion in her book *The House in Good Taste.* Her treatise, written before she married, begins with the premise "Men will always be guests in our homes." William Odom always gave his mother credit for inspiring his love and knowledge of beautiful things. Certainly Eleanor Brown believed that women were the better decorators, and didn't hesitate to say so. After she expressed her unwavering opinion in an article in the *New York Times,* one of the few men she ever hired, Albert Hadley, decided it was time for him, with grace and goodwill, to leave McMillen, Inc. Hadley's subsequent unlimited success, and the success of countless other male decorators, suggests that there may be no single answer to our question.

Jean-Michel Frank, 1934.

In 1930, Frank commissioned Adolphe Chanaux, the Paris decorator, to work with him on designs for his apartment in the rue de Verneuil. Chanaux had been trained by the top designers in Paris in the 1920s, and he was good at his craft, but up till then his taste had always been conventional.

Frank provided the inspiration that Chanaux needed to break free. Their initial collaboration on Frank's apartment soon led to a more creative venture. When Frank was nearly forty years old, the two men established a partnership and opened their first atelier in the Ruche workshops in the rue Montauban. In 1933, they opened their second shop, named simply Jean-Michel Frank, in the rue Faubourg Saint-Honoré. For Frank, the shop was more than a business; it was the realization of his lifelong search for perfection. Records and photographs show that from the start of their joint enterprise, Frank and Chanaux surrounded themselves with the most talented designers, artists, and craftsmen of their day, including Christian Bérard, Emilio Terry, Serge Roche, and Alberto Giacometti and his brother Diego. This collaborative of artists and designers worked in a manner not unlike that employed by eighteenth-century *ensembliers* or the participants in Hoffman's Wiener Werkstätte.

It is difficult, if not impossible, to determine which of the two decorators, Frank or Chanaux, played the leading role in the partnership, but one thing is sure: Frank never did any of the drawings for his own designs. He either enlisted the help of a draftsman or provided rough sketches for all of his projects. This method of designing was a technique he would pass on to Truex. Chanaux, in contrast, as a graduate of the École des Beaux Arts, was technically competent and had the professional expertise required to handle the materials he and Frank used. Chanaux had learned his trade as a cabinetmaker with André Groult, and had participated in the fabrication of the famous anthropomorphic pieces of furniture in ivory and white shagreen displayed in "Madame's Bedroom" in the French Embassy Pavilion of the 1925 Exposition. At the end of the 1920s, Chanaux had also worked for a short time in Ruhlmann's atelier but found his designs excessively bourgeois. There can be no doubt that Chanaux's experience contributed to the success of his collaboration with Frank. From Chanaux, Frank gained the technical knowledge he needed to execute his designs. A few designs have been attrib-

uted to Chanaux himself, but for the most part, he played a brilliant second
fiddle to his celebrated partner.

A success from the first, Frank and Chanaux attracted the business of
Elsie de Wolfe, Frances Elkins, and Eleanor Brown and supplied them with
goods for their decorating commissions in the United States. They also executed designs for Syrie Maugham's work in England. In addition to producing
furniture, rugs, and lighting fixtures, Frank and Chanaux were commissioned
to create interiors for Elsa Schiaparelli, Lucien Lelong, Vicomte and Vicomtesse de Noailles, and Guerlain, Inc. Later, in America, Frank would design the living room of Nelson Rockefeller's New York apartment and
Templeton Crocker's house in San Francisco. When Rosamund Bernier took
Billy Baldwin to see Frank's work in the Noailles house on the place des
États-Unis, Baldwin enthused, "I have never seen grandeur made so intimate
and everything so perfectly placed. The house should be used as a lesson in
furniture arrangement for every interior design student and every seasoned
decorator." He described the grand salon as "the pièce de résistance, Frank's
masterpiece."

Committed though Frank was to the work of Le Corbusier and
Robert Mallet-Stevens, the foundation for his contemporary design actually
lay in the style of Louis XVI. His interiors employed rare materials such as
bleached split-straw marquetry, mica, shagreen, and exotic woods, as well as
more common leather, parchment, white plaster, and lacquer. Even when
using such sumptuous materials—or *especially* then—Frank followed the advice of Madame Errazuriz and kept his rooms astonishingly spare. He believed
that one furnished a room by "unfurnishing" it. There were never pictures on
the walls of a Frank-designed room, and no accessories beyond perhaps a
Greek bust, an ancient fragment of sculpture, or a piece of primitive African
art. On seeing one such stark interior designed by Frank, Jean Cocteau joked,
"Pity the burglars got away with everything."

*Truex's apartment,
Paris, 1935.*

Not long after their second meeting, Truex invited Frank to be a visiting critic at the Paris school. During Frank's time there, his aesthetic would gradually begin to take over Truex's sense of design. What we now call the Parsons table, based on an ancient Chinese "elephant foot" design, was but one product of their collaborative work in these years; another, subtler result was the distillation of Truex's taste and sense of design, a process that would continue for the next four decades. Pictures made of his apartments in the 1950s show his growing commitment to Frank; by the middle of the 1960s, the metamorphosis was complete.

When Frank became a visiting critic, the philosophy of the New York School of Fine and Applied Arts was still entrenched in the traditions established by Parsons and Odom. Even though Odom was then in New York, he continued to dictate the content of courses and remained in complete charge of the policies at the Paris school. Regardless of how much personal freedom Truex enjoyed while he was the director of 9 place des Vosges, he knew he was there to implement Odom's programs and ideas. It was thus necessary for Truex not only to administer the school according to Odom's dictates, but also to offer outward and visible demonstrations of his loyalty. The decoration of his personal living space was the most obvious display of his allegiance: photographs of Truex's apartments in Paris and, later, of his first apartments in New York reveal that he remained true to the training he had received from

Odom. This situation had to be difficult for Truex, who was continually exposed, through his broad spectrum of new friends, to the emerging modernism in architecture and interior design. For him, these new concepts were profound ideas and not, as Odom believed, passing fads.

An even more delicate problem for Truex was the growing ethnic prejudice of some of his closest friends. Most of the wealthy people he knew belonged to "restricted" clubs and did not associate with Jews. Hitler's atrocities were not even discussed in their closed world of privilege. Just as he had known not to take Sergio Pizzoni to his American friends' homes, Truex also knew that Frank would not be accepted there. Although Frank did not adhere to any religious belief, everyone knew that he was a Jew and lived openly as a homosexual. In the truly sophisticated salons of Paris, Frank was not only accepted but celebrated.

The political unrest in Europe and the critical financial situation in the United States continued to have little impact on either the Paris school or Truex's personal life. The students who were enrolled at the New York School of Fine and Applied Arts came from families of sufficient wealth that their lives were largely untouched by the Depression. In this they were in the small-

Truex table set for lunch, Paris, 1935.

est minority: by 1932, thirty million people were unemployed in the industrial nations, six million of them in Germany alone. America's isolationism continued to be promoted by Joseph Kennedy, then the ambassador to the Court of St. James's, and Charles Lindbergh, whose popularity was without equal in the United States.

Most of the distinguished

faculty of the Bauhaus, in self-imposed exile from Germany, emigrated to America in the 1930s. Once in the United States, many went on to other educational institutions, where they were to have a major influence on the evolving modernist school of design and architecture. Josef Albers went to Yale; Walter Gropius accepted a position at Harvard and in 1939 would work with László Moholy-Nagy to establish the Institute of Design in Chicago. In Europe, the pursuit of greatness in the arts was no longer in vogue. In 1933, students at the University of Berlin had burned thousands of books, including the works of Proust, Gide, Freud, and anyone else they considered to be an enemy of the Reich. In 1937, twenty thousand visitors a day would file in to see Hitler's Degenerate Art exhibit, intended to discredit modern art, design, and architecture.

Truex's apartment, Paris, 1938.

In 1939, fearing a German invasion and the persecution of Jews and homosexuals, Jean-Michel Frank would leave Paris and, with the aid of Madame Errazuriz, find refuge in Buenos Aires. From South America, Frank would travel to the United States, where he would execute his celebrated interiors for Templeton Crocker and Nelson Rockefeller. Truex would convince Eleanor Brown to provide the money necessary for Frank to establish his own design firm in New York City, but by then it would be too late: in 1941, the tragedies of his early life and his fear of the future would drive him to take his own life by jumping out a high window in Manhattan. While there was never a Frank period in French design, as there was a Ruhlmann period, there was a Frank moment. The products of the Frank-Chanaux collaboration of the early 1930s, both individual pieces and complete interiors, created

Rockefeller's apartment, New York, designed by Frank. Furniture by Frank; carpet by Bérard; console, lamps, and fire dogs by Alberto and Diego Giacometti; painting over the mantel by Matisse; other paintings by Picasso.

an aura of harmony, a synthesis of new and traditional forms that melded with the requirements of the time.

The financial crisis of the 1930s had dampened enthusiasm for overembellished design of the sort shown at the 1925 Exposition, and replaced it with a desire for a cleaner, more restrained look. In response to the new austerity and asceticism, Frank and Chanaux developed a style that placed them squarely between the "traditionalists," as exemplified by Ruhlmann, and the "formalists," represented by Charaux and Le Corbusier.

In 1976, Truex wrote a long article for *Architectural Digest* entitled "Jean-Michel Frank Remembered." In it he raised the questions "How much of the work did Frank actually design himself? How much of it was the result of the designers and artists around him? To what extent was he a catalyst? How much of his design was due to the influence of friends and clients? Is it important to know?" In answer to that last, Truex concluded, "I think not."

On the Eve of Departure

$\mathcal{E}$ven as European political unrest continued to mount in 1937, Millicent Rogers, now married to Ronald Balcom, insisted that her mother and Truex join her and her sons for Christmas in Austria. Her invitation implied that it might be their last holiday at her chalet in the Alberg Valley. As soon as Truex arrived, she asked his advice about which of her Biedermeier antiques she should ship to America. Knowing her eclectic taste and her disdain for anything bourgeois, he urged her not to worry about editing her collection but simply to send *everything*. He further assured her that a good decorator could work out the details after the furniture got to the United States.

Christmas at the chalet was celebrated with a great flourish, though there were few prospects for a happy new year in Austria. In her imperious way, Mary Rogers demanded that no one spoil the holidays with talk of war. She was not alone in her persistent belief that the dramatic events occurring all around would not affect her little world. Even after signing the Munich Agreement on September 30, 1938, and thus leaving Czechoslovakia defenseless, Neville Chamberlain would proclaim, "I believe it is peace for our time . . . peace with honor." Prompted by Chamberlain's statement, Charles Lindbergh would write to Joseph Kennedy, "I am convinced that it is wiser to permit Germany's eastward expansion than to throw England and France, un-

Fete for the arrival of Goebbels in Venice, 1939.

prepared, into a war at this time." He would go on to add that England could not possibly win a war in Europe, even with the aid of the United States.

In June 1938, Odom paid a last visit to Paris. He gave Truex instructions about what should be done with the school's furnishings and records if it came to that. The main salon was appointed with good, though not extraordinary, antiques; if there was a war, Odom wanted them shipped to New York. He assured each member of the faculty and staff that if classes were suspended, it would be for only a short time. When he lunched with Lady Mendl, she told him his anxiety was a waste of energy, adding that she herself had no intention of ever leaving Villa Trianon. After two weeks of work and numerous appointments, Odom left for England.

By the autumn of 1938, students heading for Paris could not help but have qualms about the darkening political situation, but neither Odom nor Truex saw any reason to change plans for that academic year. By their reasoning, all of the students who were registered for classes were either in France or already on their way. The two men continued to believe that regardless of what happened, the United States would not be involved; should Germany accelerate its war efforts, students would have the security of diplomatic immunity. The great majority of French citizens certainly did not want war. Not yet recovered from the loss and grief of the First World War, France was strongly opposed to becoming entangled in any further conflict. Jean Giono, the militant French pacificist novelist, went so far as to ask, "What's the worst that can happen if Germany invades France? Become a German? For my part I prefer being a living German than a dead Frenchman." In Europe and America, blatant, unabashed anti-Semitism blamed the Jews for the political agitation and promoted the allegation that it was warmongering Jewish bankers, eager to sell weapons, who wanted to start a war. Wealthy Americans with holdings in Europe, and American corporations doing business in Germany, remained silent in the face of these accusations.

Even though the State Department advised all United States citizens to be prepared to return home, none of Truex's friends seemed to grasp the seriousness of the situation. Bettina Wilson certainly wasn't leaving her job at *Vogue,* and Louise Macy had no plans to resign from *Harper's Bazaar.* André Durst, Jean Schlumberger, Niki de Gunzburg, and Lanfranco Rasponi refused to listen to the boring talk of politics and prospects of war. All of them had work to do, parties to attend, and parties to give. Like most people, they believed that if there was a war, it would be over in a matter of days.

Classes and programs at 9 place des Vosges went on as usual through the spring of 1939. Truex would not even think about closing the school. The twelve years he had been there represented the longest stretch of time he had ever spent in one place. Since 1927, Paris had been his home. While he had enjoyed the social life, his primary concerns had always been the school, his teaching, and the welfare of his students. Odom had assured Truex that if war did break out, he would continue to be employed as vice president of the school and a member of the New York faculty. Odom's visit the previous summer had prompted Truex to consider which of his own belongings he might want to send back to New York with the place des Vosges shipment. Fond though he was of the things he had collected over the years, he knew that nothing he owned had any great value, and besides, the circumstances of his early life had fostered in him a near-total lack of sentiment toward possessions. Still, he decided that if and when the time came, he would ship his Dalí painting, a Napoleon III–period mirror, a Louis-Philippe–style needlepoint rug, a pair of small chairs, and a reproduction Roman bust; everything else in his apartment, he was prepared to leave. Having made these decisions, he moved on to sorting through and editing his own photographs, paintings, and drawings. These were the only things that truly mattered to him.

In the spring of 1939, Paris society was gayer than ever. The rich continued to indulge themselves with luncheons, garden fetes, and grand galas.

The costume balls that season, hosted by Prince Jean-Louis de Faucigny-Lucinge, Comte Etienne de Beaumont, and Vicomte and Vicomtesse de Noailles, were lavish. André Durst dazzled everyone with his famous Bal de la Forêt at his new house at the edge of the Mortfontaine, and Adrien Drian created a sensation with his Pink Library Ball. Baron Nicholas de Gunzburg, for his part, gave not one but *two* extravagant parties—his traditional Country Ball and a Second Empire Ball.

Louise Macy, meanwhile, hosted a magnificent soirée at the Hôtel Salé, now the Musée Picasso. Bettina Wilson remembers the affair as "a fabulous success that was the best surprise ball of the season." She reveled in the myriad crystal chandeliers lighted with hundreds of candles, the men turned out in "white tie and decorations," and the women dressed in "white ball gowns and tiaras," all of which produced a "festive air not known in the Hôtel Salé since the Venetian ambassador was entertained there in the eighteenth century." Not to be outdone, the Right Honorable Mrs. Reginald Fellowes hosted her Oriental Ball, and Lady Mendl ended the season with a spectacular Circus Party at Villa Trianon. This last event took ten months of preparation. Stephane Boudin of Maison Jansen decorated the party rooms, and on the day of the party, the English floral designer Constance Spry supplied three plane-loads of white cut flowers flown from London. There were three orchestras and a dance floor built on springs that made the guests feel as if they were floating. Entertainment was provided by acrobats elegantly clad in white satin, riding white ponies imported from Finland. Lady Mendl herself made her entrance on the back of an elephant.

As they had done in each of the four previous years, Truex and Pizzoni spent the Easter holiday of 1939 at Valsanzibio. At term's end, Truex was scheduled to visit friends in Italy before meeting Pizzoni in late August for a trip to the Dalmatian coast; they planned to rendevous in Monte Carlo and go from there to Dubrovnic. Mary Rogers and Elizabeth Chavchavadze both called to say they were leaving early for Venice and expected Truex to spend time with them there. He had also promised Violet Trefusis that he would come see her at Villa l'Ombrellino in Florence. And as if all that weren't enough, a few days before leaving Paris, Truex received a letter from Mrs. Charles Marshall (today Mrs. Vincent Astor) inviting him to visit her and her husband, Buddie, in Portofino. She explained that Mary Dunn, the wife of the American ambassador to Italy, had told her about him, and added that she hoped he would accept her invitation so they could get to know each other.

When Truex arrived in Venice, he found that many of his favorite friends were already in residence. Millicent and Ronnie Balcom, along with Millicent's sons, Peter Salm and Arturo and Paul Peralta-Ramos, were staying with Mary Rogers. Valentina and George Schlee, Noël Coward, Lanfranco Rasponi, Barbara Hutton Reventlow, Iris Mountbatten, and Harry Bull (then the editor of *Town and Country*) and his wife, Daphne, were all either at the Grand Hotel or in apartments they had rented for the season.

Mary Rogers, like Lady Mendl, held firm to her belief that if only no one would talk about the war, it would not happen. Her illusion was shared by most of her American friends. In a like manner, the citizens of Venice not only shut their minds to the thought of war, but also closed the shutters of their windows to avoid the sight of Joseph Goebbels when he visited their city. The highlight of his tour was a procession down the Grand Canal, with Nazi flags flying from every gondola and bridge.

In his best form, Truex entertained Mary Rogers and her family with witty conversation throughout the day and evening. Over the years, he had become so much a part of the family, and was so often with their grand-mother, that the young Peralta-Ramos boys thought he was a relative; they could not remember a Christmas or family celebration that had not included him. While Millicent Balcom had a governess to shepherd her young sons, Truex was their favorite playmate. After a couple of weeks of high-spirited

Princess Elizabeth Chavchavadze, Venice, 1951.

family fun with them and their grandmother, however, it was time for Truex to move on for his visit with Elizabeth and George Chavchavadze.

When he arrived at the Palazzo Polignac, Marian Brandini, her parents, Count and Countess Volpi, and Wally Toscanini Castelbanco were there for lunch. Truex left his luggage with the butler, knowing from previous visits that it would be taken to his room, where his clothes would be unpacked and carefully put away. This was only one of the exquisite details of hospitality he had come to expect on every visit he had made to the palazzo since 1926. Truex also knew that in his room there would be a handwritten list of the other guests who had been invited for lunch and dinner during his stay. Fresh flower arrangements and a bowl of fruit were placed in every guest's room each morning, and fresh towels delivered to his or her bathroom twice a day. Truex's room, the one he always stayed in, faced the garden. Two sets of French doors opened onto a balcony that overlooked the palazzo's enclosed patio.

Each evening of Truex's visit, dinner was served at nine on the terrace overlooking the Grand Canal. The silver and crystal on the table were antiques of superb quality. The pattern of the service plates, all antique porcelain, was different for every course. There were no flowers on the table; Elizabeth Chavchavadze preferred to use silver or crystal centerpieces and arrange flowers on tall pedestals set around the table. The flowers, like the vegetables

Chavchavadze served, were brought daily from a farm near Padua. Every meal was served by uniformed servants wearing white gloves. The food was delicious and elegantly presented but not elaborate, in keeping with the hostess's credo: "If you want to serve meals that people will enjoy, keep the food simple. People like simple food." Chavchavadze was equally adamant about the care of linens: Truex knew that when he retired after dinner, his freshly ironed bed linens would be turned down and the draperies drawn for the night. Breakfast was always served to each guest on his or her private balcony or terrace. From the day of Truex's arrival until his departure two weeks later, he was, as always, fascinated by the charm and rare taste of Elizabeth Chavchavadze, whose unique style was evident in every detail of life at the palazzo. Chavchavadze wanted him to stay longer, but he had accepted the Marshalls' invitation to Portofino.

Brooke Marshall (later Astor) on the terrace of the castello, Portofino, 1939.

On his arrival in Santa Margherita, Truex was met by the Marshalls' chauffeur, who drove him to Portofino. From there he was taken in a fiacre to the castello the couple had leased each summer since 1932. The harbor of Portofino, viewed from the top of the mountain, made for one of the most magnificent sights he had ever seen. A servant greeted him at the gate and escorted him through the vast courtyard to the Marshalls' apartment, where, on the terrace, he met Brooke Marshall, her husband, Buddie, and her son, Tony.

Completely disarming, Brooke Marshall was unlike anyone Truex had ever met. In her plain summer dress, with no pretense of high fashion, she radiated charm and refinement. Both she and Buddie had a certain reserve, but with no sense of staid formality. She invited Truex to sit with them and have something cool to drink before going to his room. This first brief conversation revealed that they had quite a number of friends in common. Buddie Marshall was particularly pleased to discover that Truex knew his dearest friend and college classmate, Cole Porter, and his wife, Linda.

Everything about the castello was simple. Nowhere in the house were there any signs of the wealth so conspicuously displayed at Trefusis's La Tour, nor any of the grand elegance of the Palazzo Polignac. And there was certainly none of Lady Mendl's pretentiousness. Truex's room was completely white, from the walls to the bed linens and the towels in the bath. There was no elaborate flower arrangement, only a small faience jug filled with wildflowers like the ones he had seen blooming along the path on the way up the mountain. The furnishings—consisting of a bed, a chair, a small chest, and a writing table—were all rustic, peasant-type pieces.

When he went down to dinner that first evening, Truex could hear the sounds of pleasant conversation coming from the terrace; the voices and laughter had the sort of soft timbre that flows freely in an atmosphere of intimacy and trust. At no time during his stay did Truex hear any rude or boisterous outbursts. He observed that Brooke Marshall's presence seemed to set the tone for perfect behavior. Whether he was having breakfast or tea on the terrace, sailing with the men, or sharing a quiet moment alone with Brooke, he always felt it was a rare privilege to be with this family. While the Marshalls could have surrounded themselves with innumerable people of note, they were not in Portofino to be entertained. In their disciplined life, everyone was up no later than six-thirty in the morning. Long walks preceded breakfast, which was followed by reading and a regimen of personal chores. Young Tony studied with his tutor while Brooke and Buddie Marshall occupied themselves with opening the daily mail, writing letters, and taking care of responsibilities pertaining to the house. Truex used his time to sketch and paint. Lunch, at twelve-thirty, was always followed by a siesta. After four o'clock, there was tennis, swimming, or sailing. Americans and Europeans who had summer houses nearby were often invited for dinner. Truex spent ten relaxed days and nights in this fashion before leaving for Monte Carlo, where he was to meet Sergio Pizzoni.

While he and Pizzoni had known many happy times together, Truex was unprepared for the indulgence of this holiday. Pizzoni had made all the arrangements, booking only the best hotels and the finest restaurants. Every day and night of their two weeks together was a celebration. And then suddenly, as if it had been a dream, the summer was over. It was time for Truex to return to Paris and open the school. On the last day of his holiday, in Dubrovnic, the newspapers reported that Germany and Soviet Russia had signed a mutual nonaggression pact. World War II had begun.

During Truex's first week back in Paris, Hitler's troops and aircraft attacked Poland. Parisians were fearful and apprehensive. On September 19, eighteen days after the invasion of Poland, France and England declared war on Germany. Two days earlier, Charles Lindbergh had broadcast his first message on American radio urging the United States not to intervene under any circumstances; his popularity had lent the speech tremendous weight. Most American citizens still believed that their country would have no part in the conflict. But regardless of the sentiment back home, Truex faced the reality of running a school in a country that was at war. Odom instructed him to close the school, see that every student and faculty member had safe passage to America, and then return to New York himself, immediately. Truex was in no way alone in his urgency: most Americans in Europe were now desperately trying to book passage home. Burnet Pavitt and John Mallet had been called back to England for military service, and Pizzoni went home to Valsanzibio, where he received orders to report for duty in the Italian navy.

At a luncheon, Truex shared with Mona Williams his pressing need to

Truex with Mona Williams, center, *and Felicia Fisk, aboard the S.S.* Rex, *1939.*

ensure that the students had safe passage home. When he admitted that he had not even thought about how and when he himself would get back to New York, she insisted that he travel with her on the S.S. *Rex.* She was sailing from Naples in the first week of October and felt confident that she could book his accommodations. The following morning, she sent a message to the school saying that everything was arranged for him to accompany her and several of her close friends. To his chagrin, some of the students refused to accept the seriousness of the political situation and, in the most cavalier manner, left for a holiday in Switzerland.

With all trains completely booked, getting from Paris to Naples posed yet another nightmare for Truex. Again Mona Williams came to his aid, inviting him to ride in her car. Just as he had arrived in Paris with a single suitcase twelve years before, now, at thirty-five years of age, he left with one piece of luggage for his clothes and a small canvas bag in which he carried his most prized possessions: his scrapbooks of photographs, his paintings, and his drawings.

When they got to Naples, they found the harbor filled with Italian naval destroyers. Ottavio and Eva Prochet, Felicia Fisk, and Peggy Healy, friends of both Williams's and Truex's, were already on board the *Rex*. Even though they all had first-class accommodations, they were aware of a certain aloofness on the part of the staff, a definite absence of the exuberant Italian spirit. Nevertheless, the American friends indulged themselves in what would be their last luxuries for a long time to come. They were returning to a country still gripped by financial depression—a nation whose government had resorted to issuing food rationing stamps in an effort equitably to feed the ever-increasing numbers of people on welfare.

Some of the most important years in Truex's life were marked by the opening of World's Fairs. The year he was born, the 1904 Saint Louis Exposition opened, and he landed in France for the first time during the 1925 Paris Exposition. Now he returned to the United States not long after ribbon was cut for the 1939 World's Fair. His reentry coincided with the arrival of another native of his home state of Kansas: a little girl named Dorothy, from the great western plains, arrived in New York City as the star of the motion picture *The Wizard of Oz*.

In the movie, after a horrific cyclone, Dorothy and Toto, her Cairn terrier, are transported to the land of Oz. Overwhelmed by what she sees, Dorothy says to Toto, "I don't think we're in Kansas anymore." This was not far from Truex's astonished reaction on returning to live in New York City again, though he felt more horror than awe: while he had heard and read reports of the financial depression, he was unprepared for the devastating realities. Ten years after the Wall Street crash, eight million people were still out of work in the United States, and there was little hope of relief. The economic plight of the American people was now compounded by fears of war.

New World

*T*ruex's abrupt departure from Paris recalled that day in Idaho many years before, when his father, without warning, had packed him up and driven him to live with Aunt Puss in Concordia, Kansas—and that other day, too, when he had to leave Concordia and rejoin his family in Rice Lake, Wisconsin. Now, after living abroad for most of his adult life, he was being forced to return to New York City. Relying on his indomitable spirit, he was determined to make his new life a successful venture.

Truex and Mona Williams had known each other for years, but their time on the S.S. *Rex* added a new dimension to their friendship. They spent many hours together at sea, and by the time they reached New York, they had developed a remarkable bond of confidence and trust. When Truex confessed that he had no idea where he was going to live, Williams insisted that he stay in one of her guest rooms until he was settled. When they disembarked, she had his suitcase and canvas satchel sent directly to her house. The Harrison Williamses' house, on the corner of Ninety-fourth Street and Fifth Avenue, had been designed by Delano & Aldrich for Willard Straight, whose wife, Dorothy, was a daughter of William C. Whitney (today the house is the uptown branch of the International Center for Photography). When the Williamses lived there, it was known to be one of the grandest mansions in New York City, filled with the best things money could buy—the finest En-

Truex's last apartment in Paris, 1939.

glish furniture, crystal candelabra, paintings by Goya, Boucher, and Reynolds, and on and on. For Truex, this would be home until the following spring.

In spite of the economic crisis in America, Odom managed to run his school at a profit. In fact, enrollment was so high that the old facilities no longer provided adequate space for classrooms and studios. Just before Truex's return, Odom had moved the school to a new building at Fifty-seventh Street and Lexington Avenue. Truex's arrival, coinciding as it did with the move to the new location, could not have been more propitious. It was the perfect moment for him to rejoin the New York faculty and establish his position as the vice president of the school.

Eleanor Brown was then the school's prime benefactor and Odom's most trusted adviser—indeed, he never made a move without her approval. Quite aware of Mrs. Brown's importance, Truex was delighted to find a welcoming note from her and an invitation to dinner. When he went to her apartment, she hastened to tell him how glad she was that he was back in New York just now, and proceeded to speak freely about some concerns she had about Odom and his recent erratic behavior.

Having known Odom since the days when she was one of his students, Mrs. Brown assured Truex that she had never wavered in her respect for him, but she felt he needed help with the organization of the school in the new facilities. It was she who had first suggested the East Side location, to put the school closer to her offices. Mrs. Brown had been responsible, too, for Odom's appointment of an advisory board, even though all the board members knew that he continued to run the school according to his own dictates. Joseph Platt and William Pahlmann, both members of the board, shared her respect for Odom and agreed that he was showing signs of being distracted. All three of them thought he exhibited a marked degree of frustration and confusion in his dealings with the students. The term "mental depression" was not commonly used then, but that was in fact what they had observed in Odom's behavior.

At the time, Odom was only fifty-five, certainly not an old man, and the few people who were close to him believed that his unusual behavior was caused by the strain of the daily operation of the school. Administration had never been one of Odom's strengths, and closing the Paris school and moving the New York facilities had definitely taken a toll on his emotions. It was widely known, too, that Odom had never had Parsons's and Truex's talent for teaching. Seemingly without meaning to be, he was frequently abrupt with the students. This behavior had become a sharp, if not bitter, note in his personality. Since England's entry into the war, Odom had seemed more acerbic than ever, though he was unable, or unwilling, to communicate what lay at the root of his uneasiness.

Eleanor Brown, on the beach, Southampton, 1944.

Mrs. Brown shared all of this openly with Truex, who she hoped would be able to provide the support Odom needed and bring some levity to the administration of the school. To her mind, his record in Paris proved that he had the leadership qualities that were now required in New York. Platt, having previously convinced Odom that Truex should head up the Paris school, was in full accord. Now famous for his motion-picture set designs—he would win Academy Awards for his work on *Gone With the Wind* and *Rebecca*—Platt had become a leading figure in American interior design, and Odom was more inclined than ever to listen to his opinions. Together he and Mrs. Brown would encourage Odom to give Truex greater responsibility for the daily management of the school.

Neither Mrs. Brown nor Odom, Platt, or anyone else realized that Truex had come back to the United States a dramatically changed man, with a refined taste and style that were uniquely his own. New York now seemed provincial to him. He found it incomprehensible that in all the years he had been away, so little could have changed in fashion, interior design, and the arts. In Paris, he had been exposed to some of the most creative designers of the century; he was shocked to discover that none of these new ideas had made even the slightest impression in New York.

One of Truex's frustrations in his teaching was the lack of original art and good examples of classical architecture. Whereas in Paris he had relied on the great museum collections and the inherent magnificence of the city, in New York he was forced to resort to poor-quality photographs to illustrate his lectures. Even with these limitations, Truex instilled in his students an appreciation for the importance of original art. He was unrelenting, too, in his insistence that nature would serve as the best source of inspiration in their design projects. Every assignment he gave required research at the Metropolitan Museum or the Museum of Natural History. He also lectured on emerging ideas in modern art and design, which added immeasurably to his popularity with his students. He frequently took his classes on gallery tours and to the Museum of Modern Art. None of his success went unnoticed by those who were championing his career at the school.

Another great surprise for Truex when he returned to New York was the food. While he always ate very little, in France he had developed a palate that went far beyond the bland fare served in America. Even at the homes of supposedly sophisticated people, the meals he was served seemed unimaginative and uninteresting. He was appalled by the enormous portions and the presliced bread offered in restaurants. He knew that if he was going to survive, he would have to cook. The lesson Elizabeth Chavchavadze had taught him—that simple food, properly presented, was fundamental to gracious living—became his touchstone. He soon discovered that June Platt shared his passion for well-prepared meals, and had even published a cookbook, *Party Cook Book,* in 1936. Their common interest in the culinary arts strengthened the bond they had established during the Platts' year in Paris.

In his years in France, Truex had become so accustomed to the male-dominated world of interior design in Paris that he had forgotten that virtually everywhere else, this work was largely the province of women. The highly skilled, extremely talented females who dominated the arena in America were known as the Lady Decorators. While William Pahlmann was head of interior design at Lord & Taylor, Ross Stewart directed the interior design department at W. & J. Sloane, and George Stacy had earned professional status working on his own, none of these men had a reputation equal to that of the best women in the field. Even Billy Baldwin still worked under the banner of Ruby Ross

Wood. One of the few who had made names for themselves as important interior decorators was James Amster, who was also touted for Amster Yard, the unique mews of shops and apartments he had created on East Forty-ninth Street.

Now almost eighty years old, Lady Mendl still considered herself the premier interior decorator in America, and as soon as she returned to the country, she set out to reclaim any authority she might have lost while living in France. In 1940, Truex's first year back in New York, Elsie Cobb Wilson's interior

Lady Mendl, Villa Trianon, 1939.

decorating firm was reorganized as Smyth, Urquhart & Marckwald; the three women who ran it were no less powerful than Mrs. Wilson had been in her heyday. Eleanor Brown's firm, McMillen, Inc., was by then firmly established as the leading and only "full-service" decorating firm in the United States.

Nancy McClelland, the founder of Au Quatrième, the antiques and decorating department in Wanamaker's New York store, was not only a respected decorator but also a published author and recognized authority on the history of the decorative arts. Truex's old friend Marion Hall, whom he had seen often in Paris with Mary Rogers, reigned supreme, with her partner Diane Tate, in re-creating the English country look for rich Americans. Dorothy Draper had been in business for fifteen years and commanded both recognition and enormous fees for her work in the corporate world. Rose Cumming might be considered an eccentric, but she was still an indomitable force in interior design. And Agnes Foster Wright, Melanie Kahane, and Mrs. Henry Parish II were the rising stars who greeted Truex on his return to New York. While Mrs. Parish's early work was done primarily for friends, she would go on to become a leading American decorator with one of the most elite clienteles ever assembled.

New York's *corps de femmes* of decorators was not unique. In Palm Beach, Mrs. Polly Jessup led the pack, as the noted architect David Adler's sister, Frances Elkins, did in California. The influence these women wielded in America was mirrored in England, where Syrie Maugham and Sybil Colefax dominated the interior decorating profession.

With the exception of Eleanor Brown and Elsie Cobb Wilson, none of these women had studied interior design, but all had an innate sense of taste. They were all well versed in French and English period furniture and extremely knowledgeable about the art and antiques markets. Their financial success demonstrated both a shrewd understanding of the marketplace and a sensitivity to clients' needs, as a significant part of the job involved catering to the desires of people who either came from old money or wanted to create the impression that they did. Since the 1876 Philadelphia Centennial Exhibition, and certainly since the opening of the American Wing at the Metropolitan Museum of Art in 1924, people of wealth and power had been demanding rooms decorated with antiques or good reproductions and comfortable upholstered furniture. Taste in decorating had remained essentially unchanged for fifty years, and the Lady Decorators were, to a woman, experts at providing what their clients wanted.

Most of the students at the New York School of Fine and Applied Arts were women eager to enter the interior decorating profession. Just as that profession had changed little in fifty years, the curriculum that the school offered had also been static. Because Truex had been the head of the school in Paris, he was labeled as a proponent of Odom's conservative attitude, but that had always been something of a double-edged sword for him. On the one hand, the school's prestige brought him into close contact with people of wealth and power; on the other, its conservative reputation made it difficult for him to move freely in the world of avant-garde designers and artists.

Jean-Michel Frank had been Truex's closest link to the elite world of new design, but it must be recognized that Frank himself was never in the mainstream of avant-garde art; rather, he created his own art form. While few people in New York society and none of the city's leading decorators cared about modern art, Truex knew that he had missed a great opportunity in Paris. During his twelve years there, from 1927 to 1939, he had never been a part of the world of the modern artists, writers, musicians, architects, and designers. Now that he was back in New York, it was too late for regrets about what might have been. Truex's immediate concerns were organizing his courses for the fall, working with William Odom, and maintaining his relationship with Eleanor Brown, who had already proved to be an infallible resource for information on the New York design world. Mrs. Brown, for her part, felt that the time was fast approaching when the New York School of Fine and Applied Arts would need a change of leadership. To her mind, when the hour came, Truex would be the man to head the school.

Zelina Brunschwig, a contemporary and close friend of Mrs. Brown's, shared her her high opinion of Truex. In her early training, Parsons and Odom had introduced Brunschwig to the world of interior design and antiques, but it was Truex who had taught her how to draw and paint. For that, she was extremely grateful. After graduating from the New York School of Fine and Applied Arts, she had worked for a short time for Mrs. Brown at McMillen, Inc., and remained fiercely loyal to her former employer. Like Mrs. Brown, she had the greatest respect for Odom but was wary of his unyielding contempt for modern design. She was aware of Truex's struggle to bring contemporary art and ideas to the school. As the head of Brunschwig & Fils, Inc., which would become one of the most prestigious fabric and wallpaper houses in America, Zelina Brunschwig believed that it was the responsibility of the designers of every age to produce work that was typical of and right for its period. Her niece, Murray Douglas, now a principal in Brunschwig & Fils, remembers that when her aunt's husband was away during World War II, she and Truex became very close friends. "Van's thoughts and ideas on design were important to her, and she relied on his opinions," Douglas recalls. She adds, "In the book on our company, *Brunschwig & Fils Style,* it is an unfortunate omission that Van is not given credit for our motto 'Good taste is forever.' I remember that Mrs. B., the pet name for my aunt, was quite proud of the fact that he wrote it." Brunschwig's (and Brown's) confidence in Truex was seconded by Grace Fakes, who had also returned to the United States in 1939 and was now a vice president at McMillen, Inc., and a guest critic at the New York school. While Truex was aware of the ambitions these women harbored for him, he remained loyal to Odom and his philosophy.

As Christmas 1939 approached, the news of the war in Europe got worse. Recent immigrants to America were frantic about family members left behind in Europe. Still, public sentiment in the United States favored an isolationist stance—a position that American corporations doing business in Germany were all too happy to endorse. In response to the atrocities being committed against Jews, the United Jewish Appeal was founded to raise money for relief, but it found little support beyond the Jewish community. Even there, to the chagrin of the UJA's founders, numerous Jews who were financially able to help ignored their heritage: after immigrating, many had reared their children as Protestants, as Catholics, or in no religion at all. In fashionable drawing rooms in New York, the Jewish situation was not discussed. A few people actually believed that Hitler's European campaign had merit.

After the fall of France, Belgium, the Netherlands, Luxembourg, Denmark, Norway, and Romania to Germany in 1940, England was more desperate than ever to enlist the strength of the United States to help stop the German domination. But neither President Roosevelt's continuing campaign for intervention nor Italy's declaration of war on France and Great Britain did much to alter American sentiments. Finally, in September, the United States government delivered fifty destroyers to Britain. Unfortunately, the hour of hope had passed.

By the time the fall term started in 1940, Odom seemed so fragile that Eleanor Brown and other members of the board wondered if he would be physically and emotionally able to both teach and provide the leadership the school needed. When news came of the bombing of Coventry, England, in November, Odom collapsed. He did not confide to Truex or anyone else what the trouble was, and accepted neither sympathy nor constructive advice. Odom's doctors ordered complete bed rest, but still he made no move to relinquish his authority. At last, when it became apparent that he could no longer carry on, Mrs. Brown demanded that he allow Truex to manage the daily operations of the school. Every morning Truex would go to Odom's suite at the St. Regis to receive his directives and orders. Odom's confinement came a few weeks before the Christmas recess, which allowed Truex and the faculty time to plan for his absence in the spring semester. But while it was obvious that Odom would not be at work—or at least not full time—Truex knew that neither would anything be done without his consent.

Just as Truex had spent his first Christmas back in New York with Mary Rogers, again, this year, he was with her and her family. At the Christmas parties he attended, there was little indication of economic depression; the food and wines served and the gifts exchanged could not have been more

lavish. This extravagance was certainly evident at the River House apartment of George and Elizabeth Chavchavadze, who had moved to New York City in 1939. Just prior to the Christmas season that year, a significant person entered Truex's life.

Through their mutual friends Alice Garrett and Pauline Potter, Truex and Billy Baldwin had been hearing about each other for years. Finally, in the fall of 1939, they had met at a party given by Gilbert and Kitty Miller. Truex was well acquainted with Bald-

Billy Baldwin at Rory Cameron's house, Le Clos, St. Jean– Cap-Ferrat, 1965.

win's reputation as a decorator, and he knew he traveled in the most exclusive social circles. In contrast to Truex, with his humble background, Baldwin had been born into a life of privilege. He was completely at ease with rich New Yorkers, whom he delighted, in turn, with his flamboyance. As Horst P. Horst would later say, "Billy was a naughty boy."

Born in 1903, Baldwin was one year older than Truex. While they were both attractive, they were physical opposites: Baldwin was extremely small—tiny, in fact—and Truex exceptionally tall. But they had similar personal traits, including extreme self-discipline and determination. Neither of them could ever have been described as casual: being well groomed at all times was a primary concern for both men. From the hour they got up in the morning, donning their dressing gowns to eat breakfast from perfectly prepared breakfast trays, until they retired at night, in beds fitted with meticulously ironed linens, they lived like Edwardian gentlemen.

Food, but very little of it, well prepared and beautifully served, was another fetish they shared. When Baldwin entertained in his apartment, he had always had a butler and a maid—unlike Truex, who did all of his own cooking and never had more help than a cleaning woman who came in once a week. An intimate lunch for four, a light supper and an evening of bridge with three friends—these were Truex's hallmarks of entertaining. Baldwin, in contrast, enjoyed inviting friends to expensive restaurants and was known for his large cocktail parties, inevitably attended by the most fashionable people in the city. Just as John Mallet and Burnet Pavitt had ushered Truex into *le tout Paris* in 1927, Billy Baldwin opened wide the doors of New York society for him in 1940.

Laying the Foundations

*W*hen Odom returned to the school in January 1941, he was unable to teach any classes and was in his office for only a few hours each week. Neither Eleanor Brown nor Truex had any idea, still, what had triggered his collapse the previous fall before. Odom, a devout Episcopalian, did confide to Truex that he was in regular contact with his friend Dr. George Sargent, the rector of Saint Bartholomew's Episcopal Church. But aside from these appointments with his parish priest, Odom saw no one. He relied more and more on Truex for the daily management of the school. Working with Mrs. Brown, and with the complete cooperation of the faculty, Truex began planning for the 1941–1942 academic year. Unable to meet the responsibilities of his job, Odom left early that spring for Long Island and did not return to Manhattan until the fall term was in session.

When Truex and Mrs. Brown visited Odom at his apartment in the St. Regis that October, they realized at once that his health had not improved. In the weeks that followed, they both did all they could to be supportive, but Odom resisted all offers of help. He spent most of his time in bed, seldom got dressed, and for all intents and purposes had become a recluse.

Early in November, Odom asked Mrs. Brown to call a special meeting of the board of advisors in his apartment. When the meeting convened, Odom announced that the time had come completely to reorganize the school. He proposed that it be restructured as a nonprofit corporation governed by a board of trustees. In honor of its founder and his revered mentor, Frank Alvah Parsons, Odom wanted the school to be renamed the Parsons School of Design. The board of advisors voted unanimously to implement his proposals. Eleanor Brown was elected president of the new board of trustees, and Truex was made vice president. Mrs. Brown wasted no time in making the necessary legal arrangements, required by the New York Board of Regents, to incorporate the school as the Parsons School of Design.

Some days after this meeting, Odom invited Truex to his apartment for dinner. This was the first social overture he had made to anyone in over a year. On the appointed evening, Truex was shocked to see how much weaker Odom appeared to have grown since the board meeting. His every gesture—even speaking—was an obvious effort. Despite his delicate condition, though, Odom could not have been more cordial and hospitable. His conversation made it clear that any differences he and Truex might have had in earlier years were now behind them. When the maid had cleared the last dishes and they were completely alone, Odom said that he had two favors to ask. Before making his requests, however, he wanted to share something with Truex that he had never revealed to anyone. He proceeded to talk about his close personal relationship with an Englishman named William Dickman. Truex had known Dickman for years and, like everyone else, had always assumed that he was a servant who worked as Odom's butler and valet. Odom confided that for more than twenty years, he and Dickman had shared a town house in Regents Park and a country home in Kent where they spent their holidays. In telling the story of their time together, Odom remained composed until he reached its sad conclusion: Dickman had been killed in the bombing of Coventry. As Truex listened, he vividly remembered that Odom's collapse had dated from his hearing the news of the German blitz. At last, learning of the loss Odom had suffered, Truex could finally fathom what lay behind his emotional and physical decline.

Odom told Truex that he had made arrangements with the Archbishop of Canterbury to be buried next to Dickman in the garden of Lambeth Palace, the primate's official residence in London. The first favor he requested was that Truex, when the time came, ensure that his burial instructions were honored. Odom said that while his sister, Mrs. George Rushmore, would be the chief beneficiary of his estate, he wanted Truex to have his prized set of four Louis XVI fauteuils and a pair of Vieux Paris porcelain lamps that he had bought on his first trip to France. His second request was that Truex remove these things from his apartment on the following day.

The next morning, when Truex returned to the St. Regis Hotel to meet the movers who were coming for the chairs and lamps, the housekeeper told him that Mr. Odom had been taken to the emergency room only a few minutes before. Truex immediately called Eleanor Brown and asked her to meet him at the hospital, where they learned that Odom had taken a turn for the worse. Over the next weeks and all through the Christmas holidays, Truex went every day to the hospital, always to be told that Odom was showing no sign of improvement.

Since October, when President Roosevelt had issued orders that any German or Italian vessel sighted in United States waters be attacked, most Americans had known that war was inevitable. The America First Committee, founded in April 1940 by prominent citizens who hoped to keep the country out of the war, had lost all credibility. On December 7, Pearl Harbor was bombed. The following day, the United States declared war on Japan.

Those of Truex's close friends who had turned their backs on world politics now faced the realities of war. Millicent Rogers's sons were too young for military service, but she and her mother were both determined to do everything they could to help. Mary Rogers was charged with a spirit of patriotism, and this year, at her Christmas party, no one talked of anything but the war effort. After the holidays, when classes resumed in January, Truex confronted the sobering prospect of the changes that the war would bring in his life. While his own chronic lung ailment made him ineligible for the draft, he knew that most of the men enrolled in the school were eligible for military service. The general state of alarm and the pressure of Odom's illness demanded all of Truex's energy.

Odom was in and out of the hospital, but his health continued to decline. He died on January 29, 1942. The collection of French and English furniture that he left was of such significance that certain pieces were accepted for the permanent collection of the Musée des Arts Décoratifs in Paris. Odom's other antiques and paintings, which his sister chose not to keep, were sold through McMillen, Inc., to establish an endowment fund for the Parsons School of Design. His art history and design resource library of more than two thousand volumes was bequeathed to Yale University. The sacred trust that Myron Taylor, Eleanor Brown, and others had in his taste was now, like a scepter, passed on to Truex.

On February 10, 1942, Eleanor Brown called a meeting of the board of trustees at which she and the other members elected Truex president of the school. Not yet forty, Truex was now head of the premier school of interior design in America. At the time, his only credentials for the job were his experience and his certificate of graduation from the New York School of Fine and Applied Arts. Mrs. Brown felt that the president of the school should have more academic distinction. Being from Missouri and wise to the heartland politics of America, she knew that Truex's home state of Kansas would be the best place to get what she wanted for him and the school. Under her supervision, letters of recommendation were written to key people, and in May 1942, Truex was awarded an honorary Doctor of Fine Arts degree from Kansas Wesleyan University. Only a few days later, at the commencement exercises in New York City, Dr. Van Day Truex was officially installed as the first president of the Parsons School of Design.

Truex came to his new position emotionally drained. For the past twelve months, he had worked under great pressures brought on by the war and the burden of Odom's lingering illness. In addition, he had suffered the unexpected blow of Jean-Michel Frank's suicide. The two people who had most influenced his work as a designer were now dead. With Odom gone, he was free to initiate his own programs of education. For the first time since his student days, he could fully explore his own ideas, and he could direct the school's curriculum. He had the complete backing of his board of trustees, of which he himself was a voting member, and the support of an advisory board comprising some of the most notable people in the design industry. His three most powerful allies and most important trustees, Eleanor Brown, Joseph Platt, and Millicent Rogers, were unfaltering in their support of his leadership.

What Truex, the board of trustees, and the faculty could not foresee was that the focus of the Parsons School of Design was about to shift. From the earliest days of the school's founding, the primary course of study had been interior design, with advertising design a close second. Fashion design, costume design, illustration, and teacher training had also been important, but none had come close to receiving the emphasis that was put on interior architecture and decoration. Now, because of the war, Paris was cut off from the rest of the world, which meant that fashion design would have new importance in New York. This development would present Truex with a completely new set of challenges and forever change the course of study at Parsons.

While its student body had always been predominantly female, during the war Parsons became almost entirely a school of women. Smaller enrollments during the war years meant that less money was available for operating

William Pahlmann in uniform during World War II.

expenses and faculty wages. Because there were no endowment funds to relieve the financial strain, Truex found himself in the difficult position of presiding over a school that had insufficient funds to pay even his own salary. Fortunately, Millicent Rogers, now serving on the board of trustees, came to the rescue. Beyond her generosity for the general welfare of the school, she also made sure that Truex and the faculty were paid.

When Truex had first returned to New York in 1939, his modest salary had not been a problem. The Great Depression had served as a social equalizer and, except for the extremely wealthy, no one had much money. Now that wartime rationing was in effect, the gap between the rich and the poor was further narrowed. Even for those with financial resources, there was nothing to buy. To meet the social obligations of his new position as president of the school, Truex developed a studied simplicity that he referred to as his ability to "distill." When an occasion demanded that he host a group larger than his customary three guests, he relied on buffet parties. Having mastered a few inexpensive casseroles, such as his Green Chicken, that could be prepared in advance, he entertained without the help of a staff. This atmosphere of informality, in which people served themselves, was something he had first experienced in the 1930s, when he visited Coco Chanel at her county house, La Pausa, in the Médoc. Whenever he was expecting a large group, he would carefully arrange the furniture in his tiny apartment, eliminating everything extraneous, to create an ambiance of simple elegance that rivaled the panache of the most stylish drawing rooms in the city. The social graces he had learned in Europe and his sophisticated wit added to his allure. With so many men away in military service, Truex became one of the most popular bachelors in New York City.

From the bombing of Pearl Harbor on December 7, 1941, until V-J day, August 14, 1945, New York City, like all of America, lived under a new social order. Women entered the workforce as every able-bodied man in the United States was either drafted for military service or assigned to a civilian relief job. Only those men with physical disabilities and those too old or too young were exempted from the war effort. While Truex was ineligible for the draft, he wanted to make some sort of contribution, so he used his connections at leading New York art galleries to arrange several exhibitions at which his paintings were sold to support war relief funds. Working with Millicent Rogers on the Medical and Surgical Relief Committee she had organized, he helped to raise money to enable the distribution of medical supplies in the war zones of Europe and Asia.

Melvin Dwork says that to his mind, Truex's greatest contribution to the war effort consisted in his writing to all of the Parsons students who had been drafted for military service. He remembers that the letters he received from Truex, full of news of the school and New York City, were extremely reassuring to him. Dwork explains, "Mr. Truex, as I called him then, kept ever before us the idea that when the war was over, we were coming back to Parsons to complete our education. These were not form letters. Every letter was handwritten and personal, meaning that he wrote to us individually about our future and our careers. Van Day Truex gave all of us hope."

Art Galleries and Great Loves

Truex had begun painting seriously when he was still the head of the Paris school. In 1936, Boutet de Monvel had arranged for his first show, at Wildenstein & Company. The *New York Sun*'s review of the exhibit compared Truex's "clarity of line" to that of Alphonse Legros, the French-born British painter who had taught at the Slade School of Art in London. Emphasizing the "elegance" of his work, the review stated, "Truex is a sound draftsman who works in an infallibly decorative manner." Finally, referring to Truex's paintings of ancient Roman statuary, the critic asserted, "There is such gusto in these renderings of super-people in marble that the suspicious may conclude that Mr. Truex may have become involved in the tremendous political exaltations that have been fermenting in the old world recently." In 1936, the implications of this comment would not necessarily have been read negatively in the United States.

On Truex's return to New York in 1939, Felix Wildenstein had made arrangements to mount another show of his work. This second exhibition was favorably reviewed in both *Art News* and the *New York Times,* with the latter reporting that Truex's wash drawings were "skillfully painted compositions," and adding, "There is much of the virtuoso in his art." While the paintings were still on display at Wildenstein, Carroll Carstairs arranged for Truex to have yet another show, at his gallery. When *that* show was reviewed in "*Vogue*

Truex ink and wash drawing, Italian Garden, *1965, private collection.*

Truex gouache and watercolor painting of two pieces of table sculpture, 1931, private collection.

Covers the Town," the writer praised the artist for creating "drawings with architectural clarity . . . distinguished for their handling of line." In his scrapbook, Truex noted that Grace Moore, Elsie Mendl, Hedda Hopper, and Dorothy Kirsten had all bought paintings at the opening.

While most of Truex's work was architectural, an *Art News* review of the Carstairs show held that "Truex's drawings of groups of nudes demonstrate his sense of sculpture. They are finely modeled in light and shade, rounded and firm in feeling as a sculptor's drawing." A newspaper review found in Truex's scrapbooks (the name of the publication is missing) is headlined "Exemplifying Elegance in Art" and subtitled "Van Day Truex Makes Protest Against Shabbiness." In the article the critic suggests, " 'Swank' is a term not often applied to works of art yet it may safely be applied to the drawings of Van Day Truex. They are in the mode, by the mode, and for the mode, and they are going to encourage heartily all those who have been pining for something definitely modish to cling to. Ownership of one of these [Truex] drawings would be paramount, I should think, to being listed with three addresses in the Social Register." This last remark was on point: many of the people who collected Truex's work *were* in fact listed in the Social Register.

Because Americans were unable to travel to Europe during the war, many of them spent their winter holidays in Mexico. On a visit there with Mary Rogers in 1942, Truex realized that the early Spanish colonial buildings would serve as an attractive substitute for the European architecture that his classes had studied before the war. On three occasions, he took groups of students to Cuernavaca, Oaxaca, and San Miguel de Allende. Reviewing the work that Truex himself did on these trips, one New York critic said, "Truex's paintings have the verve of a Chopin waltz played by Artur Rubinstein." The *New York Sun* review of the same work proclaimed, "The paintings have a succinct elegance;" the *New York Times* concurred, describing the paintings as "sure, spirited, and expert in design."

In November 1945, *Art News* published a lengthy overview of his oeuvre, entitled "Truex: Draftsman de Luxe." The writer expressed some regret

Truex still life presented to Grace Moore in 1945. The antique cup in the foreground bears the inscription "Love the Giver," private collection.

that "while Mr. Truex's worldly contacts have enormously benefitted Parsons School of Design, the confluence of his admirers at openings has in a way closed him off from the mainstream of art in America. He has that easy elegance claimed by some to be France's special birthright." He concluded with a wish: "One would like for the museums of the country to get to know Truex's work and see him take his place as a serious painter in the annals of American art where he belongs."

In November 1948, a review in the *Christian Science Monitor* of one of his shows at Carstairs would begin by saying,

Top: *Truex wash painting,* Val-de-Grace, *Paris, 1937, from the estate of Mary Rogers, private collection.* Right: *Truex wash painting,* Dubrovnik, Yugoslavia, *from the estate of Barbara Hutton, private collection.*

"Because Truex has a facility in capturing the spirit of different architectural traditions, particularly that of the lively and expansive baroque, and of rendering them softened and harmonized by the effect of brilliant sunshine, he has been called the poet of city churches." Summing up, the reviewer inferred, "Truex deliberately cultivates informality, casualness, unusual perspective, and off-center design. He achieves his success by believing that freshness of approach and capturing of the spirit, rather than the form, are the essential things." The year before, in 1947, a review in the *World Telegram* had praised Truex's "exceptional skill and unfailing taste."

The 1950s and 1960s would bring more changes of venue. After showing at Carroll Carstairs's gallery until 1954, Truex would be invited to show his work at the Maynard Walker Gallery, on East Fifty-seventh Street. Fourteen years later, Truex would, at the urging of the art dealer Robert Graham,

move to the Graham Gallery, at 1014 Madison Avenue. The *New York Times*'s April 1954 review of his exhibition, at the Carstairs Gallery, asserted, "Truex is at his best when dealing with architecture. He sets temples and churches and biscuit-shaped villages receding in a firm perspective as logically as the pieces in a chess set. Clarity is Truex's forte and his work is buttressed with natural taste." He recorded in his scrapbook that Mrs. Lewis

Truex wash painting, Pilgrim's Roadside Marker, Ménerbes, France, 1960, private collection.

Lapham, Mrs. Wolcott Blair, Mrs. Nathaniel Potter, Mrs. Ottavio Prochet, Mrs. Vincent Astor, and Mrs. Alfred Vanderbilt were among those who bought paintings at this show.

In 1955, Truex had a one-man show that opened at the California Palace of the Legion of Honor in San Francisco and moved from there to the Santa Barbara Museum of Art. In both cities, the show received critical acclaim. Alfred Frankenstein's review in the *San Francisco Chronicle* said, "These works are vigorous, fully developed, and self-sufficient. The line is crisp, tense, and brilliant. Logic and spontaneity are beautifully balanced here. The whole show is rich and mature in craftsmanship and imagination." In 1970, two of Truex's paintings, *French Village* and *Italian Mountain Village,* were acquired for the permanent collection of the National Gallery of Art in Washington.

There can be no doubt that painting was one of the great loves of Truex's life. He gave tirelessly of himself to his art, kept photographs of nearly all of his works, and maintained a meticulous record of his exhibits. The people he loved or gave himself to are a decidely different matter; only two such are clearly identified in his scrapbooks and writings.

At Mary Rogers's last party in Venice in the summer of 1939, Gladys Swarthout had told Truex that she very much wanted him to meet her best friend, Grace Moore. At the time, Swarthout, Moore, and Lily Pons were the reigning prima donnas of New York opera. Moore was also known for her roles in Broadway musicals and her success in Hollywood films. In 1942, soon after Truex was elected president of Parsons, Swarthout invited him to a party along with Moore and her husband, Valentin Parera. As Swarthout had anticipated, Truex and Moore immediately liked each other: their introduction was reminiscent of the reunion of two old school chums. Although their lives were completely different, they shared a curious commonality. Each had grown up in a middle-class family and had a father who worked in retail, and both were mavericks who, at about the same age, had cut their small-town ties and come to New York City—Truex as student and Moore to star in her first Broadway hit, Irving Berlin's *Music Box Review.*

When Moore heard about the challenges Truex was facing at Parsons, she asked her friend Condé Nast to help. Nast already knew Truex and was fascinated by his expanded fashion curriculum at the school. Responding to Moore's request, the publisher instructed all of his editors to promote both Truex and Parsons. Richardson Wright, editor of Nast's *House and Garden,*

Clockwise from top left: *Truex wash drawing,* Oppède-le-Vieux, Provence, *1963, The Maynard Walker Gallery, New York, private collection; Truex, wash drawing,* Gordes at Noon, Provence, *1963, The Maynard Walker Gallery, New York, private collection; Truex wash drawing,* Joucas, Provence, *1963, The Maynard Walker Gallery, New York, private collection.*

Grace Moore, 1943.

was already a member of the Parsons advisory board and had regularly featured the school and Truex in his magazine.

Following the Nast mandate, Margaret Case at once began championing Truex and Parsons in the pages of *Vogue*. While working with Case, Truex developed close ties with the magazine's art director, Alexander Liberman. The notices in *Vogue* in turn prompted Carmel Snow to tout the school and its president in *Harper's Bazaar*. The prolific publicity, all well deserved and hard-earned, contributed immeasurably to Parsons's reputation.

Grace Moore also invited Truex to visit her in Hollywood. Through his longtime friend and fellow Parsons alumnus Gilbert Adrian, Truex already knew many people in the motion-picture community. Adrian, then the celebrated head of costume design at MGM, and his wife, Janet Gaynor, Twentieth Century–Fox's biggest star and the winner of the first Academy Award for best actress (in 1928), included Truex in their elaborate parties whenever he was on the West Coast.

It was through Adrian that Truex met George Cukor, the famed film producer; Bill Haines, the silent-film idol who became Hollywood's much-sought-after interior decorator; and Clifton Webb. His friendship with Cukor afforded Truex the opportunity to renew old ties with one of his former Paris friends, the photographer George Hoyningen-Huene. When planning a trip to southern California, Truex always scheduled a visit with Sir Charles and Lady Mendl at After All, their home in Beverly Hills, and made certain that his itinerary allowed him some time with his long-cherished friend the interior decorator Frances Elkins, at her Casa Amesti in Monterey.

Truex's ventures to the West usually also included a stopover in San Francisco to see his friend, and former New Yorker, Whitney Warren. To escape the shadow of his famous father, the architect who designed Grand Central Terminal, Warren had moved to California, where he had become quite successful growing and marketing almonds. Although he never really needed the money, his estate, Bear River Ranch, was a serious and lucrative business. As one of San Francisco's leading patrons of the arts, he would later arrange for Truex's two California exhibitions.

His visits to San Francisco also enabled Truex to stay in touch with another former New York friend, Anthony Hale, in his opinion one of the two best young decorators on the West Coast (the other was Michael Taylor). It

Truex watercolor drawing, Edgewater, Hudson River, estate of Richard Jenrette, private collection.

was at Tony Hale's apartment that Truex met Hale's client Richard Jenrette, a partner in the New York investment firm Donaldson, Lufkin and Jenrette. The young broker's passion for buying and restoring old houses fascinated Truex, and their introduction in San Francisco led to a long friendship in Manhattan, with Truex frequently visiting Jenrette at his two houses, Edgewater on the Hudson River and Roper House in Charleston, South Carolina. Jenrette remembers, "Van was an older man when I met him. He was the perfect houseguest, always very entertaining. When he came for a visit, he knew all of the latest gossip, but I never heard him say a bad or mean thing about anybody. I remember thinking that Van's stories were great fun but never malicious."

Despite Truex's myriad connections in California, spending time with Grace Moore was always his first priority. He also frequently visited Moore and her husband at their farm, Faraway Meadows, near Newtown, Connecticut. Without fail on these occasions, immediately upon his arrival, Moore would present him with a list of decorating projects she wanted done around the house. Her admonition was, "Van, don't bother asking my opinion. Just do what you think is best. I'm a singer. You're the decorator." In her autobiography *You're Only Human Once,* Moore described Truex as "one of the most talented people I ever knew." The admiration was mutual: totally fascinated by Moore, Truex went to all her New York openings. When she starred in *Tosca* in Montreal, he and Whitney Warren traveled to Canada with Parera for the premiere. At the party following her opening performance of *Louisa,* in San Francisco, Truex confessed to Warren, "Grace is the sweetheart I never had."

Following Moore's tragic death in a plane crash in Copenhagen in January 1947, Truex, Warren, Clifton Webb, the Cole Porters, and the Gilbert Millers would be among those who would organize her memorial service at Riverside Church. More than five thousand people would come to the service to remember her. Moore had always remained faithful to her Southern Baptist heritage and attended church regularly, and in acknowledgment of her devotion, Dr. Harry Emerson Fosdick would deliver the eulogy, Dr. Robert McCracken would read the Scriptures, and Virgil Fox would play the organ. To honor both Moore's legacy to American music, especially at the Metropolitan Opera, and their friendship with her, Dorothy Kirsten and Lawrence Tibbett would sing. Before the memorial service in New York City, Truex would accompany Parera to Moore's funeral and burial in Chattanooga, Tennessee.

One of the few things Truex kept his whole life was a scrapbook full of clippings about Moore's career and articles on her death and funeral. Included in the book is a small menu from a Christmas luncheon that he attended with Clifton Webb, hosted by Moore, Gladys Swarthout, and Lily Pons at Chateaubriand in New York City in 1945. Truex always kept Moore's picture in his apartment and owned all of her recordings. His friend Isabel Roberts remembers, "When we visited Van in Provence, after dinner, often he would put on one of Grace Moore's recordings. When she was singing, no one was allowed to speak. This was more than twenty years after she died. He absolutely worshiped her."

The other person who completely captivated Truex during these years was a young man named Sheridan Kettering. In September 1942, Kettering enrolled in the interior design program at Parson, only to be drafted for military service a few weeks later; after failing the physical examination, he returned for classes. Kettering was one of the few men who graduated from Parsons dur-

Sheridan Kettering, Mexico, 1945.

ing the war. Extremely handsome and always beautifully attired, he unfortunately had a moody nature and an uncontrollable temper. While he could be
absolutely charming, he could also be ruthlessly demonic. His mercurial
mood swings, which came without warning, were accompanied by uncon-
strained outbursts of bad behavior during which he was completely devoid of
manners. In spite of Kettering's often loutish actions, Truex doted on him.
People who knew them both and were close to the situation remember that
Truex was mesmerized by Kettering from his first day at Parsons, even though
the younger man openly reviled him, accusing him of being overbearingly
formal and pandering to Mona Williams, Mary Rogers, and her daughter,
Millicent. Kettering was also intolerant of his relationship with Grace Moore.
Finally, he disliked Eleanor Brown and thought Truex should confront her and
make it clear that she did not run the school. To Truex's chagrin, Kettering did
not hesitate to say all of these things in public.

  According to one of New York's most respected decorators, "Kettering

*Truex and Diana
Vreeland with Mark
Mooring and Jo
Copeland at the
annual student fashion
show, Parsons School
of Design, 1944.*

had an innate gift for decorating. Even the best designers envied him. His remarkable talent was evident from the day he entered the school. Van immediately became his champion and was always ready to defended his brutish behavior. In response, Kettering was unbearably cruel to Van." After graduating from Parsons, Kettering was offered his first professional interior design position at the firm of Melanie Kahane, a job that Truex had arranged. Later he established his own business in New York City and enjoyed a moderate success, but his behavior became more and more erratic. He frequently left town in the middle of a decorating job, giving no explanation to his clients or vendors, and did not reappear for months. During these tumultuous years, Truex continued to see him. If he had hoped to foster a relationship with Kettering like the one he himself had had with Parsons and Odom, he was disappointed. Eventually Kettering would move to Massachusetts and open a small decorating shop on Cape Cod. In the 1960s, he would become fascinated by motorcycles and the life-style that often went with them. One of the few people who kept up with him says, "Bud, as he was called, finally ended up in California and eventually gave up decorating altogether. In 1996, I received word that he had died." After Kettering left New York, Truex confided to one of his friends, "The only people I ever really loved were Sheridan Kettering and Grace Moore.

The Years of Intrigue

Before Truex's return to the United States in 1939, an article in *Vogue* had referred to him as "the best-known American in Paris." Publicity such as this paved the way for his later reputation as the most elegant and stylish man in New York, and the consistently good reviews accorded his art shows only added to his appeal. Every prominent hostess in the city wanted Truex at her party. During the war years, he was a frequent weekend houseguest of friends in New England, going on many occasions to visit Brooke and Buddie Marshall at Milne House, their vacation home in the Berkshires, and, with Mona Williams, to Cole and Linda Porter's farm in Williamstown, Massachusetts. He was a regular visitor, too, at the Willows, the Cape Cod home of his Chicago friends Charles and Isabella Goodspeed. Through his close ties with Mrs. Norman Whitehouse and Eva and Ottavio Prochet, he was also invited each summer to be a part of the elite community, known as the Bailey's Beach crowd, in Newport.

Although Joseph and June Platt lived a much simpler life than most of his other friends, Truex often stayed with them at their small cottage in Little Compton, Rhode Island. In Connecticut, he spent time not only with Grace Moore but also with Valentina and George Schlee and with the Gilbert Millers, at their Great Ring Farm. His scrapbooks show that many of his weekends with Moore included visits with another of his favorite families, the

Vreelands—Reed and Diana and their two sons, Timmy and Frecky. From Vreeland's earliest days at *Harper's Bazaar,* beginning in 1939, throughout her editorship of *Vogue,* from 1962 until 1971, and continuing into her years at the Costume Institute at the Metropolitan Museum of Art, she and Truex were devoted friends. The respect they had for each other was no doubt enhanced by their shared friendships with Billy Baldwin, Millicent Rogers, and Whitney Warren, and by their fierce opinions on matters of style and taste.

The snapshots in Truex's scrapbooks from the war years comprise a veritable photographic record of the *New York Social Register.* On Long Island, he was often with Archibald and Eleanor Brown at their home, Four Fountains, in Southampton; with Myron and Anabel Taylor at their Underhill Farm, in Lattingtown; with Mrs. George Blumenthal at her house, La Lanterne, in Brookville; with Mrs. Louis Jacques Balsan (formerly Consuelo Vanderbilt and later the Duchess of Marlborough) at her estate, Oldfields, in Oyster Bay; and with Millicent Rogers and her family at the H. H. Rogers Southampton estate, Port of Missing Men. After America entered the war, he also went often with Rogers to Claremont Manor, her Tidewater estate in Virginia. On one of his first visits there, she commissioned him to decorate the house to accommodate the Biedermeier furniture that she had shipped back from Austria (on his advice) in 1938. Each winter, Mary Rogers and Jimmy Donohue, the Woolworth heir, both invited Truex to join the fashionable enclave in Palm Beach. To emphasize his inclusion in her family, Rogers referred to the guest house on the grounds of her estate, Thatchcote, as "Van's Cottage." Wherever Truex went, from New England to Florida, he promoted Parsons School of Design and became proficient at raising monies to support the school's scholarship fund.

During the war and in the years that immediately followed, relying on social connections and working with Billy Baldwin and Mrs. Brown, Truex gained entrée for his classes into some of the great private homes in New

Truex snapshots of a weekend with Linda and Cole Porter in Williamstown, Massachusetts. Clockwise from top left: Linda Porter (with umbrella) and Mona Williams; Cole Porter; Cole's Cottage; The Great House, home of Cole and Linda Porter.

York, on Long Island, and in Connecticut. The students enjoyed the unique advantage of their teacher's personal relationship with the owners of the houses, the architects who had designed them, or the decorators who had planned the interiors (more often than not, he knew all three—owner, architect, and decorator). Long before the great duPont estate, Winterthur, became a public museum, for example, Truex was a frequent guest of the owners, Mr. and Mrs. Henry Francis duPont. He was familiar with their collection of American antiques, just as he knew intimately the collections of Jules Bache, George Blumenthal, and Robert Lehman. The trips he arranged for the interior design students extended to Pennsylvania, Virginia, Georgia, South Carolina, Illinois, and Wisconsin. With the help of Frances Elkins, he was able to arrange for groups of students to see many of the houses that her brother, David Adler, designed on the North Shore of Chicago and in the suburbs of Milwaukee. After the war, classes from Parsons visited Philip Johnson's Glass House and other important modern houses built in New Canaan, Connecticut. Each year, too, Edgar Kaufmann, Jr., one of Truex's closest friends, made arrangements for students to tour his family's Frank Lloyd Wright house, Fallingwater, near Pittsburgh. When these field trips were initiated, few of the houses that the students gained access to were open to the public. Their privileged visits were not unlike the opportunities that Odom had provided for Truex when he was a student. But whereas Truex had gone alone on his early excursions, or with Odom, the trips he planned for his students included the entire class.

After the war, a great change took place at Parsons: while the school had always been respected, it now became an educational phenomenon. By 1947, Truex's untiring efforts had helped Parsons earn an international reputation as the best interior design and fashion design school in the world. The leaders of the American fashion and interior design industries, anxious to be a

part of it, readily served on boards, gave special lectures, and generously contributed monies for programs.

    During World War II and in the years that immediately followed, Paris
was forced to relinquish its place at the center of the fashion world (the focus
would shift back only when Christian Dior presented his first collection,
"The New Look," in 1947). In these same years, the ready-to-wear industry
in the United States flourished, producing uniquely American designs. The
New York designers had an enormous influence on casual clothes, and major
department stores played a key role in the promotion of fashion. It was during
this period that Dorothy Shaver, the legendary president of Lord & Taylor, became one of Truex's major supporters and joined his board of trustees. Adam

*The senior student
presentation of interior
design projects:* left to
right, *Frances Elkins,
Eleanor Brown, and
Truex, New York
City, 1950.*

Gimbel, the president of Saks Fifth Avenue, and his wife, Sophie, became two of the school's most generous benefactors. In the same spirit of cooperation, the fashion designers Jo Copeland, Mark Mooring, Claire McCardell, and Gilbert Adrian (all graduates of Parsons), as well as Norman Norell and Elsa Schiaparelli, all contributed to the development of the school's new fashion curriculum. The top figures in the fashion publications industry also lent their talents to Parsons, with Diana Vreeland, Alexander Liberman, Margaret Case, and Carmel Snow all agreeing to serve on the school's advisory board.

William Pahlmann, having returned from military service and resumed his position as head of interior design at Lord & Taylor, was anxious to do all he could to support his alma mater and his friend Truex. George Stacey, also a Parsons alumnus and one of the most important decorators in New York, served as the school's senior interior design adviser. George Nelson and Raymond Loewy, both of whom Truex knew well and greatly admired, played key roles in developing Parsons's postwar courses in interior design. With the advent of new materials following the war, the emerging building and home-furnishings industries in the United States and the recovering countries of Europe were generating new products and enormous revenues. Leaders in the home-furnishings field, including Florence Knoll, worked generously with Truex to plan the curriculum required to meet the changing needs of the interior design profession. In 1949, Truex would serve as one of the official U.S. representatives to the acclaimed Milan Triennial, later to become the International Show of Italian Furniture and Design.

Under the direction of Milton Glaser, Bradbury Thompson, and Paul Rand (a former Parsons student), the course known as Advertising Art was completely restructured and renamed Graphic Design. In this period of flux, the architect William Adams Delano and William Katzenbach and Franco Scalamandre, two of the most respected fabric and wall-covering manufacturers in America, remained loyal supporters of the school. Embodying the spirit of the old guard, they made sure that the traditions of Frank Parsons and William Odom were not lost.

During this time of extraordinary growth and ferment at Parsons, the entire student body routinely assembled for Truex's lectures. In an article published the October 1999 issue of *Elle Decor,* Kenneth Paul Block, the celebrated Parsons-trained fashion illustrator, remembered, "When Truex entered the lecture hall, we were all spellbound. He was so supremely elegant to look at that it didn't really very much matter what he said." While none of Truex's class notes or syllabi have survived, we know from existing school catalogs that he systematically taught in every department and lectured to the whole school on a regular basis. Charles Sevigny, the Paris-based international decorator and former Truex student, says:

> *Van could be talking about William Kent, Charles Le Brun, or how to make an omelette, and everyone in the class was inspired. I distinctly remember that when we were given an assignment that related to a historical period, such as the eighteenth century, he insisted that our work [be] based on original art forms. Once I was at my drawing table looking through some shelter magazines, like* House and Garden, *you know, and he came by and asked what I was doing. When I said I was getting ideas for an assignment, he was furious: "Go to the source for ideas, go to the Metropolitan Museum, find your inspiration in nature, go to the Museum of Natural History, but never rely on something that someone else has done." His mandate has stuck with me. Today I don't subscribe to a single decorating magazine, but I do collect old and rare books on architecture and design. Van instilled in us a sense that only the best will do. Nothing second-rate.*

Truex's apartment,
New York City. On
spread, clockwise,
from top left: *1944;*
1946; 1949; 1951.

The only written record of Truex's dictums while he was at Parsons is "Mirrors of Personality," a lecture given at the Decorators Club in 1942 and published in *Interiors* that same year. Renderings of the apartments of Bernard Boutet de Monvel, Elsa Schiaparelli, Diana Vreeland, and Lady Mendl are used to illustrate his theories. The text begins with the pronouncement "Interiors speak!" and then moves from place to place, from room to room, asking the reader to understand that "rooms emphasize whether one exists or lives, and there is a great difference between the two!"

Truex, in this essay/lecture, stresses, "The modern scene in decoration is not a unified or controlled one. The unified control of the arts during the reign of Louis XIV no longer exists; today the designer is free to achieve a wider variety and more personal approach to the interior." He warns, however, that "this can produce extremes of the very good and the very bad— rooms stripped of all proportion; sofas and armchairs designed in such a manner as to leave one in doubt whether to sit or to sprawl; and over-charged, over-romantic rooms that belong to the theater[,] not to the house." He explains, "The combination of an individual [i.e., a client] with a positive idea of living and a good designer is the great force in contemporary decoration. I don't care how good the designer is, I am sure that he [or she] would rather have a person with definite ideas rather than have to work with a negative figure as a client." To convey one of his most deeply held convictions, he borrows a quotation from Gertrude Stein's *Paris France:* "France has scientific methods, machines and electricity, but does not believe that these things have anything to do with the real business of living. Life is tradition and human nature."

Truex seizes the opportunity to emphasize his distaste for pseudo-period rooms: "There is nothing more trite than a period room imposed on a contemporary setting. And when I say this I want you to know I am not questioning the splendid, beautiful rooms in old houses. They were made for the house. What I am questioning is the setting of a previous era, resembling something out of a museum, in a New York City apartment. We do not want trite reproductions. A late eighteenth-century room seen in Aix-en-Provence with its lovely toile-de-Jouy on the walls, with its provincial furniture, does not look so well and is far from appropriate when it is reproduced in [apartment] '16B.' " The lecture ends with a plea for quality: "My voice is one of many that must be raised to combat this unfortunate trend in present-day living. Better rooms, better furniture, better objets d'art can only be created for a society interested in living—not existing."

Truex's unwavering opinions, born of his Parsons teaching, would be aired again in the 1970s in a series of articles for *Architectural Digest*. He cautions that "overlighting in public or private places can be as bad as underlighting—both made possible by the advances in techniques. . . . These new fixtures: *spots, cans, shaded wall appliqués* can get out of bounds." Better, here, to be conservative: "There is no denying that the well designed table lamp provides a quality of light in a private room not to be had otherwise." For dining, he advocates the creation of a "festive atmosphere," and finally proclaims that "the magic of candlelight, the most subtle of all, is an exquisite addition to any and all lighting."

In another article in the series, "Responsibility in Design," Truex tackles the tough question What is taste? and offers his own definition: "The ability to notice, appreciate, and judge what is beautiful, appropriate, harmonious or excellent; a sense of beauty, excellence and fitness." In all of his writing, he is consistent in his preference for the term "design judgment" over the word *taste*. He explains that design judgment can be learned or developed, whereas "flair is a keen natural sense of discernment, a natural talent or ability that cannot be taught. One has it or not. Flair added to taste [design judgment] pro-

Nicholas de Gunzburg, left, *and Truex at Harold Guy's home, Strawberry Hill, in Flemington, New Jersey, 1946.*

duces the top creative work." In this same article, he deplores what he calls "outrageous embellishments" and warns that "price is not the determining factor in achieving true quality."

In "Reproduction Furniture: The Pros and Cons," Truex keeps an open mind on the matter before him. After quickly denouncing the so-called Provençal and phony Medieval and Renaissance styles as "so much rubbish," he suggests that certain reproductions are perfectly acceptable. He cites as an example line-for-line copies of dining chairs made to complete a set of twelve when there are only five originals. Nor does the fact that his own service of Royal Worcester china, "Blind Earl," is a copy either bother him or detract from his pleasure in using it. He finds reproductions of Edwardian chintz, William Morris wallpaper, and African fabric patterns, among others, completely correct and concludes with the pronouncement, "The criterion for using reproductions should be the quality of design."

Two of Truex's *Architectural Digest* columns were written in deference to his most cherished mentors. "The Magic of Mirror" recalls the favorite decorating device of William Odom, while "A Journey to India" extols the virtue of Near Eastern decorative motifs, reflecting Rory Cameron's passion for Indian colors and designs. Three of his articles, "The Public Look versus the Private Look," "Private Rooms," and "The Pleasure of Scrapbooks," take as their central theme one of their author's most touted principles: the need for the client's individual character to be evident in the interior design. In "Scrapbooks," Truex intones, "pretentiousness illustrates what I most dislike in interior design." In the same article, he turns to another favorite topic: "Any designer who does not appreciate or know about good food is not a very good designer. The planning of a meal and its presentation—the texture, the color, the tastes, the hot and cold temperatures—are the same concerns that affect an environment." Never hesitant to reveal his predilections and opinions, he cites the designers and decorators he most admires throughout his articles for *Architectural Digest*. While Odom is frequently mentioned, he consistently reserves his highest praise for Billy Baldwin.

An important shift occurred in the school with the enrollment of GI's returning from the war. These men brought a new level of maturity to Parsons, and the G.I. Bill meant they had money to pay their fees and tuition. The student body, previously dominated by women, now encompassed a large number of men who wanted to learn interior decorating, fashion design, costume design, and fashion illustration. Between 1945 and 1950, applications for admission poured in. To ensure adequate classroom and studio space, it became necessary for the school to lease a warehouse in Long Island City, in which all first-year classes would be taught.

During this period of phenomenal growth at Parsons, several new faculty members were hired. One was Stanley Barrows, a former student of both Odom's and Truex's and a graduate of Washington and Lee University and Parsons. According to Barrows, he had only recently returned from military duty in Europe when, quite by accident, he ran into Truex on Fifth Avenue.

His old teacher wanted to know what his plans were and whether he had a job yet. When Barrows confessed that he had neither plans nor a job, Truex hired him on the spot and told him to report for work the next morning. While Barrows's joining the faculty would prove to be a real boon for Parsons, another appointment that Truex made soon after that would give him cause for regret. The man's name was Harold Guy.

Truex had been introduced to Guy by Niki de Gunzburg, and he thought he was one of the most naturally talented interior decorators he had ever met. Guy had had no formal training as a decorator but had developed a remarkable eye while traveling in Europe in his formative years with his wealthy mother. When Truex met him, Guy had a private income that relieved him of any necessity to work. He had, in fact, never had a job of any kind and instead spent most of his time decorating his house, Strawberry Hill, in Flemington, New Jersey.

In the years immediately following the war, Eleanor Brown and her staff at McMillen, Inc., were swamped with new commissions. To free herself from the constant pressures that the school imposed, Brown in 1948 appointed her husband, the architect Archibald Manning Brown, to Parsons's advisory board. Almost immediately, Archibald Brown nominated Hamilton Preston to serve as the board's chairman. An employee of the school since 1935, Preston managed the daily operations, a job that entailed purchasing supplies and maintaining the facilities. He was not a member of the faculty, nor was he ever privy to management policies. Over the years, however, he had developed some unrealistic ambitions and resented having been passed over for the presidency in favor of Truex. When he was elected chairman of the advisory board, he became quite outspoken in his opinion that Truex spent too much time on social pursuits and lacked a vision for the future of the school.

Archibald Brown also invited Clarence Sprague, a professor of decorative art at New York University, to join the advisory board. Accustomed to a regimented style of administration that he did not find at Parsons, Sprague openly criticized the way Truex managed the school. Making matters worse was a very public swipe taken by T. H. Robsjohn-Gibbings, then a leading decorator and furniture designer in New York, who included a scathing passage on the type of interior design taught at Parsons in his book *Good-bye, Mr. Chippendale.* Robsjohn-Gibbings declared that Elsie de Wolfe and all who followed in her train (a classification that surely included Truex) were an impediment to modern design. Fortunately, Truex still had the support of Eleanor Lambert, Carmel Snow, Sara Pennoyer, Gilbert Adrian, and Alexander Liberman, all members of the advisory board.

The previous year, in keeping with her belief that the school needed the best leadership possible, Mrs. Brown had invited her friend and client Arthur Houghton, Jr., the chairman of Corning Glass, to be a trustee. Even though Truex was also on the board, Mrs. Brown clearly ran the show. Houghton accepted the invitation on the condition that his friend Pierre Bedard, chairman of the French Institute and a longtime member of the Parsons advisory board, also be made a trustee. Unfortunately, Houghton, like Hamilton Preston and Clarence Sprague, did not share Mrs. Brown's fondness for Truex. He questioned the man's priorities and his judgment. Houghton would be especially appalled when, in 1951, Truex attended Carlos de Beistegui's lavish Fête des Fêtes at his Palazzo Labia in Venice. The much-publicized event recalled the costume balls of Paris before the war and was reported to be the most expensive party ever given. For Houghton, the extravaganza was an inexcusable excess; in his mind, Beistegui was a Nazi sympathizer who had built his palatial Château de Groussay, outside Paris, while collaborating with the Germans. When Mrs. Brown defended Truex and commended his gifts as a teacher, Houghton was skeptical.

With Mrs. Brown's prompting, Houghton decided to sit in on one of

Truex's lectures. He happened to pick a day when the topic was fashion illustration. After reviewing the works of Carl Erickson, Paul Iribe, Georges Lepape, Marcel Vertes, and Rene Bouché, Truex concluded his discourse by extolling the talents of his friend Christian ("Bebe") Bérard. In Houghton's opinion, Bérard was a bohemian drug addict—certainly not the kind of person who ought to be lifted up as an example to the students. In conversations with Mrs. Brown, Houghton continued to find fault with Truex. He often referred to his own alma mater, Harvard, and made innuendos about Truex's lack of a university degree. To further emphasize his dissatisfaction with the programs at Parsons, he frequently cited the course of studies directed by Walter Gropius at the Harvard School of Design. Mrs. Brown tried to counter his criticism with accounts of Truex's success in securing financial aid for struggling students, but to Houghton, that was merely a sign of just how badly the school needed an endowment fund.

Aware that criticism of his performance was mounting, Truex proposed to the board (of which he himself was still a voting member) that he be allowed to hire an administrator who would serve as his assistant, reporting directly to him and working under his authority. He even went so far as to nominate his old friend Geoffrey Gates for the position. Truex felt certain that Gates was someone he could completely trust. They had first met in 1936, when they were both weekend guests at Grace Bingham's villa in Cannes. Truex had attended Gates and Bingham's wedding and had been with him when she died. He had also been present when Gates subsequently married his third wife, Louise Macy Hopkins.

Born into a socially prominent family, Gates had attended prestigious New England schools and had all the hallmarks of an elitist. Extremely handsome and always immaculately, expensively attired, he was known around New York City as a financial consultant. He was just the kind of man Truex thought he needed. He knew that Gates was good with numbers and could handle the business aspects of the new job. But what Truex failed to consider was that mysterious loyalty to old school ties which Gates and Houghton shared. Both of them believed that being educated at a New England preparatory school and attending an Ivy League college were vital to a man's success in New York.

When Truex had first outlined to Laurance and Isabel Roberts his plan to hire an assistant, they had begged him to find another solution to his problems. There were no two people whom Truex respected and admired more than the Robertses, who seemed to him to represent the pinnacle of integrity. Before the war, Laurance had been the director of the Brooklyn Museum. After he was drafted for special-intelligence work in Washington, his wife was appointed the museum's director pro tem, a position she would hold for the duration of the war. During those years, while continuing to live in New York City, she had been active in contemporary-music circles and close to the composers Samuel Barber, Aaron Copland, Virgil Thomson, Gian Carlo Menotti, and Francis Thorn. The Robertses also knew all the important people in the art world, including Alfred Barr, and were regular guests at the avant-garde salons of Muriel and John Draper and Kirk and Constance Askew. (Askew then ran the New York branch of Durlacher Galleries, the London Old Master dealer and one of the most important international art galleries.) Shortly after the war, Laurance Roberts had been appointed director of the American Academy in Rome. Truex spent part of every vacation with the Robertses. He not only respected them but also shared a great bond of affection with them. Laurance Roberts was firm in his advice to Truex: he should not give an administrative title to someone who could undermine his authority. He knew from his own experience at the Brooklyn Museum, and now at the American Academy, that in any organization, there could be only one boss. But Truex would hear none of it; he assured Roberts that Gates was one of his most trusted friends.

The board of trustees agreed to hire Gates, but with a caveat that Truex was not expecting. The description of Gates's new position specified that he would report not to Truex, as president of the school, but rather to the chairman of the board of trustees. This chain of command would have been awkward under the best of circumstances, and the present situation was considerably less sanguine than that. Things got even more complicated after Mrs. Brown resigned in 1949 as chairman of the board. She was nearly sixty years old, and her business demanded more and more of her time.

Under the guidance of Arthur Houghton, the board of trustees in 1950 elected Lawrence White, of the architectural firm McKim, Mead & White, to succeed Mrs. Brown. At the time, White had been a board member for only one year. As soon as he became chairman, he nominated Geoffrey Gates to be a trustee and appointed him executive vice president of the school. Although he had been at Parsons for less than one academic term, Gates now fully shared in the administration of the school and was directly involved in all policy decisions. Neither White nor Gates had any appreciation of or interest in the traditions begun by Frank Alvah Parsons and William Odom, and certainly neither was an educator. White's only concern was the legal responsibility of running the school. Gates, essentially an accountant, undertook an in-depth study of the books, which revealed that finances at Parsons were handled in a very casual manner. Nothing illegal or improper had ever been done, but few records were kept, and there was little or no accounting for expenditures and expenses. When Truex realized that the school was slipping from his control, Laurance and Isabel Roberts's advice rang in his ears.

To make matters even worse for Truex, Millicent Rogers now resigned from the board due to illness. She had been Truex's anchor and the school's most generous donor; anything he had asked her to do for Parsons, she had happily done. Even though she had been living in Taos, New Mexico, since

1947, she and Truex had remained extremely close. To symbolize their friendship, when she began creating her celebrated gold jewelry, she made an over-
size pinkie ring for him. He referred to the ring, the only piece of jewelry he
ever wore, as his talisman. When he lost it, in Italy in 1950, he told Laurance
Roberts that it was a sign of even greater losses to come.

Perhaps the only good thing that happened to Truex during this period
was having Albert Hadley, a returning veteran, enroll in the interior design
department. Immediately after his graduation, Truex hired him as a member
of the interior design faculty. Hadley was too new to be privy to inside gossip
and had no idea that Truex was under any pressure. From the day he arrived at
the school, he was devoted to the man; "Mirrors of Personality," the article
that Truex had written for *Interiors* in 1942, had been the deciding factor in his
decision to study at Parsons. He fondly remembers, "When I met him, I
thought that Van was the most elegant man I had ever seen. As a teacher, he
was the ultimate arbiter of taste."

The new chairman of the board, Lawrence White, did little more than
establish legal policy and lay the foundations for his successor. He provided
none of the visionary leadership that Eleanor Brown wanted for the school.
Although no longer the board's chairman, Mrs. Brown nonetheless remained
its most influential member. Dissatisfied with White's performance, she
pressed Arthur Houghton to take over the chairmanship himself. Houghton
agreed, but only on the condition that certain changes be made before his
term began.

It would take three years to carry out Houghton's plan, but in the end,
under Lawrence White's direction, each of his objectives would be accomplished. The first requirement was to strip the school's president and vice president of their membership on the board. To Houghton's mind, the people in
those positions reported to the trustees, and it was highly irregular for them to

serve as board members. The second mandate was that Truex be removed as the president of Parsons; Houghton felt that his entrepreneurial skills were inappropriate for the type of management he envisioned for the school. Finally, Houghton had decided that Pierre Bedard should take Truex's place. He was convinced that Bedard's experience as president of the French Institute and his long association with the Parsons advisory board made him the right man for the job. Houghton also saw him as a potential fund-raiser who could establish the much-needed endowment fund.

None of this, of course, was conveyed to Truex. In an attempt to gain support within the school, he promoted Harold Guy to head the interior design department. Only five years before, he had asked Guy to be a guest lecturer at the school, and shortly thereafter invited him to be a member of the faculty. It was the first job Harold Guy had ever had. In those formative days of their friendship, Truex, Fulco di Verdura, and Niki de Gunzburg had frequently visited Guy at his house in New Jersey, and on more than one occasion, Truex and Guy had vacationed together on Fire Island. Having always been free with his praise for Guy's talents and abilities, Truex was confident that he could count on his loyalty. Unfortunately, he soon discovered that that was not one of Harold Guy's virtues. Once Guy became head of the interior design department, he immediately aligned himself with Pierre Bedard and endorsed Houghton's poor opinion of Truex.

Truex had always dreamed of having all the departments of Parsons in one place, not scattered in various locations around the city, as they had been for the past several years. Faculty and students alike longed to have their classrooms and studios under one roof. Working under tremendous pressure, Truex thought that a consolidation of the school's facilities might ease some of Houghton's criticism. When a suitable piece of real estate came onto the market in the fall of 1952, Truex acted quickly, taking an option on the sixteen-story building at 67 West Forty-seventh Street, just one block south of

Rockefeller Center. On his own authority as president of the school, he signed all the necessary papers.

When Houghton heard what Truex had done, he asked Gates to do a feasibility study of the proposal. Gates had no choice but to report that if Truex's bid was accepted, it would bankrupt the school. After Gates submitted his findings, Houghton called for Truex's immediate removal, and in December 1952, Truex was notified that he was being relieved of his position as president of the school. Less than a year before, in recognition of his work in France, he had been awarded the Chevalier de la Légion d'Honneur. But evidently Arthur Houghton did not have *le bec fin* to appreciate his talents.

When the Parsons School of Design opened for the fall term in 1953, Houghton was chairman of the board of trustees, Pierre Bedard was president, and Truex was listed in the school catalog as a consultant. Over the summer, Houghton had hired Geoffrey Gates to work at Corning Glass. Mrs. Brown and Joseph Platt, the only members of the old guard left on the board, had persuaded Houghton and Bedard to offer Truex the title of director of European studies. It was a meaningless honorific, since the Paris school had never reopened after the war; what European study there was at Parsons amounted to little more than extended field trips.

Now out of a job, Truex knew that his future would to some extent depend on how he handled himself during the termination process. He was sure he would have no further dealings with Arthur Houghton or Pierre Bedard, but he did not want to damage his ties to Mrs. Brown or Joseph Platt. Knowing that the proposed title, director of European studies, had been their idea, Truex accepted it. When the school year ended, in the spring of 1954, his career at Parsons was over.

As soon as he was free, he went to Rome, where Laurance Roberts had offered him a nonstipendiary position as "artist in residence" at the American Academy. Truex was now fifty years old. Still mourning the death of Millicent

Rogers the year before, he received word just before he left New York that his mother had died. Roberts remembers, "When Van arrived in Rome, he was the saddest, most broken man I had ever seen."

Truex had the summer to prepare for his position as consultant to the fellows at the American Academy and to begin the healing process he so desperately needed. Hurt though he was, he had the presence of mind to realize that it would have been impossible for him to work with Arthur Houghton and the new board. While he had loved the school for more than thirty years, Truex knew he was not sympathetic to the direction Houghton had set for Parsons's future.

Not once did he seek pity from Isabel and Laurance Roberts. To them and all of his other friends, Truex exhibited an astonishing inner strength. He painted every day throughout the summer and produced some of his finest architectural compositions. When fall came, he plunged into his consultations with the fellows, impressing everyone at the academy with his adaptability. When evaluating the fellows' work and offering constructive criticism, he was at his best. He wrote to his friends in America to let them know that his appointment at the academy was for one year only and that after that he would need a permanent job. Finding the appropriate position was going to be difficult. Everyone who had seen him work with his students at Parsons said he was a brilliant teacher, but he did not want to go from the presidency of Parsons to a mere faculty position at another school. Some friends suggested that he devote all of his time to painting and drawing, but he knew he could not succeed in the postwar New York art market: his very traditional style was in no way compatible with the then-popular abstract expressionism.

Knowing that Truex had decorated for many of his friends, including Mary and Millicent Rogers and Millicent's sons, Isabel Roberts proposed that he open his own interior design firm. His response was that he did not think he could bear constantly dealing with indecisive clients. Later she learned that he did consult with Billy Baldwin about having his own decorating business, but Baldwin, fully understanding his friend's nature, advised him against it. As Baldwin would explain to Roberts, "Van is an excellent interior decorator, the best, but the business requires compromises that would be impossible for him to make."

When his term at the American Academy came to a close, Truex told the Robertses, "Whatever the future holds for me, it is not in Europe." He had decided to return to New York City. Many of his European friends had died, and others were now living in America. Sergio Pizzoni worked for an Italian corporation and maintained an apartment in Washington, D.C. After the war, he and Truex met once, briefly, in New York.

Truex had been reared on a Horatio Alger philosophy of honesty, cheerful perseverance, and hard work. In that same spirit, he now prepared to go back to the United States. When he had first arrived New York, in 1923, the hit song had been "Nobody Knows You When You're Down and Out." He knew that sentiment had not changed and felt it was paramount for him to seem confident and look good. Before leaving Rome, he used some of his savings to buy new custom-tailored suits and several pairs of handmade shoes. When he stepped off the ship in New York City in 1955, he had never looked better.

The year before, after Truex left for the American Academy, Harrison Williams had died, and his widow, Mona, had remarried Count Edward Bismarck, the grandson of Germany's Iron Chancellor. Knowing that Truex was returning to the United States with very little in financial reserves, Mona had invited him to stay with her and Eddie, as the count was called. On one of his first nights back, she gave a dinner party for him and invited his best friends as well as some other people she thought he should meet. That evening he was seated between Mona Bismarck, on his left, and, on his right, his longtime friend Isabella Chapman, the Chicago heiress, formerly Isabella Goodspeed.

Throughout the evening, Isabella and her husband, Gilbert, talked enthusiastically about Truex's accomplishments at Parsons and asked many questions about his year at the American Academy. All of his friends were embarrassed about the way he had been treated at Parsons and wanted him to get a job that would make full use of his talents. Gilbert Chapman was no exception. Before leaving the party, he told Truex he would be calling him to discuss an idea that he and his wife had about Truex's future.

Soon after Truex's return, Pauline Hoving telephoned to invite him to join her and her husband, Walter, for an *intime* Sunday lunch. Both Hovings had worked with him during his tenure at Parsons, and Walter also had long-standing professional ties to one of Truex's closest friends, William Pahlmann. Before establishing one of the most important decorating firms in New York, Pahlmann had been the head of interior decorating at Lord & Taylor when Hoving was president of that company. On the appointed day, throughout the luncheon and well into the afternoon, Hoving talked about his plans for Tiffany & Company, the venerable New York retail institution he had just acquired. More than once he mentioned that there might well be a place for Truex in his new venture. As Truex was leaving, Hoving asked him to come to his office the following week.

Late in the afternoon, when Truex returned to Mona Bismarck's and reported on the luncheon, his hostess was delighted to hear about his prospects for a job at Tiffany's. After they discussed the possibility of his working with Hoving, Mona Bismarck told Truex that she had a homecoming gift for him. Before making her presentation, she said she was aware that during his years in New York City, he had lived, from time to time, in apartments belonging to other people. To avoid embarrassing him, she added that she knew his situation was not entirely unusual: everyone knew that many wealthy New Yorkers owned apartments that they never used and that they made available, usually free of charge, to friends. Such arrangements did mean, however, that if the owners or some member of their family needed the apartment, the friend would have to find somewhere else to live. On several occasions, Truex had faced the inconvenience of having to move quickly.

Bismarck told him that she thought the time had come for him to have a place that was his own, and she presented him with a check for an apartment. She stressed that there were no restrictions on her gift: he was to buy whatever he wanted, and when he found the right place, if the check was not sufficient, she would make up the difference. Her gift represented the most security Truex had ever known—and certainly more than he had known since leaving Parsons.

Before his appointment with Hoving at Tiffany's, Truex received a phone call from an advertising executive asking if he would be interested in working as a stylist on a promotional campaign for a national carpet manufacturer. Truex did not realize that the man on the other end of the line was a former student of his, the one he had asked to leave Parsons. He now owned one of the largest advertising agencies in New York City.

Uncertain about Hoving's proposal, Truex accepted the man's offer. Later that week, when he went to the advertising agency, he still did not recognize his former student, and the man did not mention the incident at Parsons. Truex did a masterful job as a stylist, and the client requested that he be hired for additional work. Several weeks later, when the ad man called him about future assignments, Truex said he had taken another job. They never spoke again.

The advertising executive agreed to be interviewed for this book on the condition that his name be withheld. During our conversation, he had only the highest praise for Truex: "The man was a genius. He walked into our photography studios and took over. Everyone did exactly what he told them. The sets he designed were magnificent." When asked if he had any regrets about being forced to withdraw from Parsons, he responded, "Why should I?

I went on and did what I had to do. I've made a few bucks. In fact, I've made millions. Maybe it would have never happened if I had stayed at Parsons." Had he ever wondered whether Truex had asked him to leave the school because he was Jewish? "Of course not. A lot of Jewish kids went through Parsons. Some of the biggest names in the fashion business, interior design, and advertising are Jewish, and a lot of them are Parsons graduates." He returned to his encomium:

> *Truex was an inveterate teacher. All of the important designers today— Albert Hadley, Joe Braswell, Tom Britt, Angelo Donghia, the partners Richard Callahan and Eddie Zajac, Robert Bray and Michael Schaible, and Betty Sherrill—were influenced by Truex. If he wasn't directly involved in their training, he was responsible for the kind of education they got at Parsons. The same is true in fashion. Carrie Donovan, who was the* New York Times's *fashion editor, and Claire McCardell and Donald Brooks, two of the biggest names in American fashion design, all came out of Parsons when Truex was there. In addition to being a great educator, the man had flair, taste, style, authority. He had it all. There was nobody like him. After he left, the Parsons School of Design almost went under.*

Pierre Bedard's term as president of Parsons would be short-lived; after five years, a new man would be hired for the job. Like Bedard, he would stay for only a brief period, and the school's finances would continue to decline. Albert Hadley had resigned from the faculty the same year Truex left. Harold Guy's position as head of the interior design department was terminated in 1955; nine years later, the department itself would be dissolved. The original concepts of Frank Alvah Parsons would be expunged and replaced with a new course of study in "environmental design." In 1965, Stanley Barrows and the other members of Parsons's former interior design faculty would be hired to develop a program at the Fashion Institute of Technology. In 1969, with Parsons on the verge of complete backruptcy, David Levy would become the school's president. Under his leadership, it would enter into an affiliation with the New School for Social Research (now the New School University). Twenty-eight years after its dissolution, in 1992, the interior design department would be reestablished at Parsons.

If Truex ever harbored any bad feelings or resentments about his termination at Parsons, he didn't show them. The circumstances of his early childhood had taught him to put the past behind him and never to agonize over what might have been. He never uttered any criticism of either Houghton or the board of trustees and continued to speak of the school with great affection. In 1978, when a reporter from the *New York Times* asked him about his years at Parsons, Truex would reply, with ineffable modesty, "My greatest achievement was being a catalyst, provoking people to do things I could not have possibly done myself."

The Grand Manner

When Truex arrived for his appointment at Tiffany's, it was obvious that Hoving had prepared for their meeting. After a tour of the store, over coffee in his office, he told Truex that their shared friend William Pahlmann had enthusiastically recommended him. In his diplomatic manner, Hoving let Truex know that he was aware of the Parsons incident involving Arthur Houghton, and added that whatever had happened with Houghton was irrelevant to his plan for him at Tiffany's. Having worked with Truex on several projects when he was at Parsons, Hoving knew of the important relationships he had built with New York fashion designers, interior decorators, and leading department stores. He ended his references to the school with sincere praise for the things Truex had accomplished there. Most impressive to Hoving was the visionary program he had set up with New York University in 1944, which allowed students to attend Parsons for four years rather than the customary three, take courses at NYU, and earn a Bachelor of Arts degree. This was a great bonus for those who wanted to enter the teaching profession.

Turning to the matter at hand, Hoving said that he was very much in need of the taste and judgment that he was sure Truex would bring to Tiffany's. He further added that he felt Truex's European experience could

Twelve dinner plates from china patterns commissioned for Tiffany's during Truex's tenure as director of design. (See page 182 for complete descriptions.)

Previous page: Top
row, left to right:
"Marbleized,"
Hammersley Porcelain;
"Blue Celestial,"
Royal Worcester;
"Decor Schwarz,"
Tiffany Private Stock,
Le Tellec. Second
row, left to right:
"Countess de
Gignan," Augarten
Porcelain; "Hong
Kong Bird," Coalport;
"Black Bamboo,"
Hammersley Porcelain.
Third row, left to
right: *"Plaid," Royal*
Worcester; "Mosaic on
Greystone," Spode;
"Duke of
Cumberland,"
Nymphenberg. Fourth
row, left to right:
"Independence," Royal
Worcester; "Floral
Armorial," Coalport;
"Black Dragon,"
Royal Worcester.

contribute greatly to the success of his work. As they talked, it became clearer and clearer to each of them that they had a very similar sense of style. A love of beautiful things was inherent in both men. When Hoving finally broached the specifics of the job, he said that Truex's title would be director of design, and that he would be in charge of design for all Tiffany merchandise other than jewelry. He also emphasized that Truex would be an outside consultant, not a regular employee of the corporation. When Hoving had finished outlining the job, Truex asked for two concessions.

First, he wanted to be sure that he would be free to accept other design commissions; second, he wanted to live six months of the year in New York and six months in France. Hoving agreed to permit him other commissions so long as they did not encroach on any designs done exclusively for Tiffany & Co. And he thought Truex's idea of splitting his time between New York and Europe represented a definite benefit for Tiffany's, as the six months abroad would afford him opportunities to develop relationships with foreign vendors. Hoving's financial package included a consultant's fee, all travel expenses, and an extremely generous entertainment allowance, but no company benefits. The two men shook hands on the agreement.

That evening, when Truex returned to Mona Bismarck's, he shared with her the working agreement he had made with Walter Hoving and said that he planned to use her gift to buy a house in the south of France. He had wanted to live in Provence since his first visit there with Alice and John Garrett in 1930; now it would provide the ideal location from which to make business trips to Italy, Spain, and Portugal for Tiffany's. Because she and her husband were now spending most of their time at their home on Capri, Villa Il Fortino, Mona Bismarck was delighted with Truex's decision. Little did he know that his purchase of a house in France would have to wait for seven years.

Soon after Truex's appointment with Walter Hoving, Gilbert Chapman

Truex on a trip to Provence with Alice and John Garrett, 1930.

telephoned to set a date for their meeting. Reluctant to discuss the details of his proposal over the phone, Chapman would say only that what he and Isabella had in mind could be lucrative both for Truex and for Chapman's corporation, the Yale & Towne Manufacturing Company. Since Isabella Chapman was one of Truex's oldest friends, his meeting with her husband was much more personal than the one with Walter Hoving had been. Chapman came quickly to the point, explaining that Yale & Towne had long since dispensed with any aesthetic considerations in designing its products: doorknobs, hinges, and locks. Hoping to remedy that, Chapman wanted Truex to work with his engineers on producing a new line of products. Astounded by Chapman's proposal, Truex confessed that he knew nothing about hardware and protested that this was not a job for him. (There was a logical relationship between the two in his mind: one of the major components of his success had always been his careful avoidance of situations in which he did not think he could excel.) Chapman argued that Truex's years in Europe had given him the exposure and knowledge the project required. Truex again declined, saying

Alice Garrett on the
steps of her home,
Evergreen House,
Baltimore, Maryland,
1939.

that he was not interested in designing European-style reproduction hardware. Chapman, not a man to be denied, countered that he envisioned not reproductions but a line of products that would be completely new and original. This got Truex's attention.

Insisting that he could not take on the full responsibility himself, Truex suggested organizing a consortium of designers and artists to work on the project. Rather than rely on industrial designers, he proposed commissioning celebrated artists, architects, and sculptors. This was exactly what Chapman wanted. Truex promised to draw up a proposal within the month. Knowing that the Tiffany job was going to occupy most of his time, he immediately set about contacting people he thought would be right for the Yale & Towne project. At the time, neither he nor Chapman imagined that it would be more than a year before the work was completed. Nor did Truex realize that the execution of the designs would require him to make innumerable trips to Birmingham, England, where the prototypes were to be made.

The finished designs would be heralded by the press as works of modern art. Innovative and beautifully crafted, they were first shown at the Wildenstein Gallery in New York in May 1956. From New York, the exhibit moved on to Chicago, Detroit, Los Angeles, and San Francisco. The *New York Herald Tribune* reported that the hardware, executed in unconventional materials such as Venetian glass, rare woods, Italian marble, gold, silver, and bronze, was "distinguished" and "revolutionary." Isamu Noguchi, Jacques Lipchitz, Philip Johnson, Fernand Léger, Andréa Spadini, and Truex himself were among the designers of the new door pulls, knobs, and escutcheons. After reading the laudatory reviews, Walter Hoving was even more convinced that he had hired the right man to be his director of design. However, when he offered his congratulations on the success of the "hardware show," as it came to be called, Truex once again insisted that he knew nothing about merchandising. As always, Hoving assured him that he was not to be concerned with what would and would not sell; his job at Tiffany's was to oversee the creation of tasteful and beautiful objects, and nothing more.

As Truex began his new job at Tiffany's, he remained in regular contact with Burnet Pavitt and John Mallet, who were still living in London. Regrettably, nothing in their work brought them to America. Similarly, Laurance and Isabel Roberts's duties at the American Academy kept them in Rome; aside from their annual visit, they were seldom in the United States. Billy Baldwin now became more important than ever in Truex's life. The two men spoke every day on the telephone. Nothing ever pleased either of them more than having the praise and admiration of the other. Baldwin's book *Billy Baldwin Remembers* includes a glowing tribute to Truex and his work at Parsons. After noting Truex's "demanding taste," "great sensitivity," and "belief in simplicity and sincerity," Baldwin asserts, "Under his leadership Parsons blossomed into a brilliant place of learning. . . . The vitality of the school was positively energizing." In addition to Baldwin, two other men were integral to Truex's world: Walter Lees and Rory Cameron. While he was much older than either of them, they both had a significant influence on his life.

Lees had been highly honored and decorated by the British government for his military service on the staff of General Mountbatten during World War II. After the war, he had served as an attaché to the British ambassador to France before establishing himself as an international public-relations executive. Through his important clients and assignments, he became a leading figure in the postwar society of Europe, which put him in a position to be Truex's social mentor in that milieu. Lees and his vast social and business networks gave Truex entrée to the same world of privilege he had known before the war.

Cameron, with his innate taste and style, became the person responsible for the ultimate refinement of Truex's talents. The gifted young designer helped him assimilate all he had learned from Frank Alvah Parsons, William Odom, Elsie de Wolfe, Elizabeth Chavchavadze, and Jean-Michel Frank. Through his close association with Cameron, Truex would gain a confidence that would further cement his reputation as an authority on matters of design. It was this confidence that prompted Priscilla Chapman to say in the *New York Herald Tribune,* "When it comes to the question of taste, Truex is splendidly opinionated, emphatically outspoken, and dead right."

From his first days as a student in New York, Truex had been extremely guarded about his personal life, studiously avoiding people or situations that could be the subject of tabloid journalism. When he began working for Walter Hoving, in 1955, he was more cautious than ever before. It was the era of the McCarthy investigations, which targeted not only enemies of the state—that is, Communists—but also homosexuals (then called homophiles) in the military. The reports of McCarthy's efforts drew strong negative attention to the homosexual community in New York City. Truex knew full well that Hoving would not stand for anyone even vaguely suspected of any impropriety to be associated with Tiffany's. Hoving undoubtedly had some idea of Truex's sexual preference, but he never asked questions that might elicit answers he did not want to hear. In his world of proper Episcopalians, such personal matters were not discussed. Truex was acutely aware that the same was true for the women who regularly included him in their parties and celebrations. While he was invited into the elite social circle in part because he was bright and delightful company, he was also invited because he was single.

Truex's adherence to the unwritten norms and values of the society to which he aspired did not come without a price. Brooke Astor often asked him to her parties but remembers him as being "one of the saddest men I ever knew." She describes Truex as "always charming and debonaire, but there was something that I would call lonely about him. It showed in his face. Even so, he was every lady's favorite *cavalier servant*."

Dorothy Hirshorn recalled, "When Bill [Paley] and I first met Van in Italy, I was aware that he lacked something or someone in his life. Years later, when I worked with him on committees in New York, he still had a hollow, what you might call anxious, look. He made every attempt to appear happy-go-lucky, but from a woman's point of view, his smiles were empty." Brooke Astor and Dorothy Hirshorn were not the only ones to make such observations. Hard though Truex worked to maintain an image of complete assurance and satisfaction, those closest to him were never fooled. Truex compensated for the absence of a significant other in his life by giving himself totally to his work at Tiffany's. Like Hoving, he was fascinated by the fact that postwar America wanted to own beautiful things of the sort it had been denied during the years of rationing. Hoving was keenly aware of the buying power this represented. While he did not intend to compromise any of Tiffany's elitist reputation, he had definite plans for attracting the money of the affluent middle class. Working with the top public-relations firms in New York, he kept the store's name in every leading newspaper and magazine, developed the image of "the Tiffany Touch," and convinced the world that the best things in life came in Tiffany's signature blue boxes. Truex was very much a part of creating this mystique. One of his most memorable contributions to the success of Hoving's venture came soon after he was hired, when he introduced his new employer to an old friend, the French jewelry designer Jean Schlumberger. The following year, 1956, Schlumberger and his partner, Nicolas Bongard, sold their New York shop to Hoving and agreed to sell Schlumberger's jewelry exclusively at Tiffany's.

The vision that Hoving and Truex had for the store was greatly enhanced in 1958, when Truman Capote wrote *Breakfast at Tiffany's*. When the book was made into a movie starring Audrey Hepburn, in 1961, Tiffany & Co. was elevated beyond its former status as an American institution: in the eyes of the world, it had suddenly become a romantic fantasy. Truex's arduous work on the arrangements required for sequences filmed at the store resulted in a close friendship with Capote, who would later include him in the select guest list for his famous Black and White Party, held in the Grand Ballroom of the Plaza Hotel in 1966. The invitations specified that everyone was to come dressed in black and white (meaning tuxedos for the men) and wearing a mask. The affair took on an extravagance reminiscent of that of the great costume balls given in Paris before the war. Every leading socialite and noted personality in the arts was invited, as were a number of figures prominent in the political arena, since the guest of honor was Katharine Graham, the publisher of the *Washington Post*. Those who were *not* invited found some reason to be out of town on the evening of November 28. Women spent thousands of dollars on dresses designed specially for the party. Amid the other guests wearing ingenious masks, many of them originals by Adolfo, Truex and Billy Baldwin made a splash in exotic silver unicorn masks designed for them by Gene Moore.

After the death of Mary Rogers, in 1956, Helen Hull, the first wife of

Vincent Astor and the widow of Lytle Hull, became the most important woman in Truex's life. Helen Hull was a principal benefactor and patron of many of the city's music programs. Until her death, in 1976, her New York town house and her country home on the Hudson, Locust II, served as sanctuaries for Truex and her select group of other talented friends. On one visit to Locust II, Truex met the writer John Richardson, who was spending the summer in Hull's guesthouse. After this chance introduction, the two men established a friendship that Richardson describes as "never close. Frequently, more often than not by chance, we were at parties given by mutual friends. Professionally we were in different worlds. At the time I was working at Christie's, and I was certainly aware that Van's talents and abilities were held in the highest esteem. He was very well regarded in the most exclusive circles of New York City."

Following the divorce of Nelson and Mary Rockefeller in 1966, Truex would also develop a close relationship with Mrs. Rockefeller. Her cousin

Laurance Roberts remembers that she, like Helen Hull, was extremely fond of Truex, and frequently invited him to her apartment for dinner. Other good friends were John and Nancy Pierrepont, then living in Short Hills, and Lewis and Jane Lapham of Greenwich, all of whom were active in the young society of New York. Both couples readily made Truex a part of their elite set. The Laphams' devotion to him

Tiffany hostess table setting by Brooke Astor.

is evident in the telegram they would send when the show of his paintings opened in San Francisco: "No matter how much they love you, and they will, it will never be enough. Our dearest love. Jane and Lewis."

As Walter Hoving had predicted, Truex used his social connections to promote Tiffany's. In 1957, he inaugurated a series called the Hostess Table Setting Shows, which would become a semiannual fixture on the social calendar for the next twenty years. Prominent society ladies were invited to use their own silver and china, Tiffany merchandise, or a combination of the two to create table displays. The openings of these shows were widely publicized and quickly evolved into New York social events. Whenever Tiffany's announced the opening of a Hostess Table Settings Show, the public would come in droves to see how the privileged class dined. Looking at tables designed by socialites such as Mrs. John Pierrepont, Mrs. Lytle Hull, Mrs. Vincent Astor, Mrs. Angus Lightfoot-Walker, and Mrs. Lewis Lapham allowed people to fantasize about the private lives of the very rich. The Hostess Table Settings Shows were such a hit that Truex soon introduced another series, this one called the Interior Decorator Table Settings. Sister Parish, Albert Hadley, Eleanor Brown, Mario Buatta, Joseph Braswell, James Tillis, Stephen Mallory, and of course Billy Baldwin were all invited to design Tiffany tables. Truex's keen eye for talent led him to ask Andy Warhol, then a fashion illustrator, to design a table for a children's birthday party. The success of the table-settings ventures was recorded in Truex's book *Tiffany Table Settings,* published in 1960. A second volume, *New Tiffany Table Settings,* published in 1981, gave further evidence of the longevity of its author's grand scheme. Jacqueline Kennedy Onassis, the editor of the second book, said on many occasions, "We could have never produced the book without Van. His ideas and refined taste were finally what made it a reality."

While the Tiffany table-settings shows were created long before anyone ever conceived of a decorator show house, they set the standard for the myriad show houses that would follow. The tabletop shows, like the openings of William Pahlmann's showcase rooms at Lord & Taylor and, later, Barbara Darcy's model rooms at Bloomingdale's, were gala events in New York City. Unveilings of window displays at prestigious stores were also glamorous occasions, with people actually scheduling sidewalk strolls to view the windows at Bergdorf Goodman, Bonwit Teller, Saks Fifth Avenue, or Lord & Taylor on opening night. The most popular displays were always the ones that Gene Moore designed for Tiffany's: whenever a new one was due to be unveiled, people stood in line to see the magic Moore had wrought. Newspapers and magazines published feature articles on Moore's Tiffany windows, and two large volumes, *My Time at Tiffany's* and *Tiffany Windows: The Art of Gene Moore,* record his ingenious designs. Truex had no responsibility for Moore's windows, but the two men had a mutual admiration and shared in the excitement of the early Hoving years at Tiffany's. As Moore said, "Van and I knew what we were doing. There was never a committee involved in our work."

Since the end of the war, New York City had become the new capital of the world. As Jan Morris notes in her book *Manhattan '45,* the old capitals were battered and impoverished. London and Berlin had been nearly destroyed; Paris and Rome were humiliated and discredited. In America, the prodigy of the West, people were hungry for glamour. During the wartime years, the average citizen had been able to save one quarter of his income; by war's end, the liquid assets of the American people—over $140 billion— amounted to three times the entire national income for 1932. A quarter of a trillion dollars was waiting to be spent on consumer goods. After years of wartime rationing, Americans had an insatiable appetite for elegance. Basking in the spoils of victory, they were ready to buy luxurious wares. And at 727 Fifth Avenue, Tiffany & Co., Walter Hoving and Van Day Truex were ready to make their dreams come true.

Tiffany & Co.

*T*he first thing Hoving did after he took over Tiffany's was have a clearance sale to get rid of everything that did not conform to his taste. It was the first such event in the history of the company, and it was referred to by the employees as the Great White Elephant Sale. Once the things that Hoving did not want in the store, such as silver plate and leather handbags, had been removed, he and Truex set out to provide the proper background for the Tiffany renaissance.

Under Truex's supervision, the store was completely redecorated. The rows of glass cases were replaced with tables, and the yellow walls were painted a pale mauve, a variation on "Truex Beige." Working with Bielecky Brothers, Inc., Truex and Billy Baldwin adapted a Jean-Michel Frank woven split-reed chair for use throughout the store. From Eaglesham-Graf, Truex commissioned a bamboo-pattern fabric, "Brighton Your Pavilion," designed by one of his former students, Joseph Braswell, for the window draperies. Today, nearly fifty years later, Truex's original design for the store remains in place. While some of its component parts have been refurbished, the Truex Beige, the Baldwin-Truex chairs, and the Braswell bamboo fabric are all as he intended them.

Truex's passion for simple, beautifully presented meals prompted his dictum "No one can be a good designer who does not understand the prepa-

Previous: *Tabletop set
with Truex-designed
items: "Drabware"
dinner plates;
"Drabware" Liverpool
jug and dolphin
candlesticks; Italian
faience-covered server
with trompe l'oeil eggs
and plate with trompe
l'oeil olives; Tiffany
"Bamboo" flatware
and Tiffany "All-
Purpose" wineglass;
Baccarat "Dionysus"
decanter. The Franzini
sculptures in the center
of the table, entitled
Diving Boys,
belonged to Truex.*

ration and presentation of delicious food." Armed with that credo, he began his work in Tiffany's china department. His first task was to rid the store of what he called "boring" patterns, which for him encompassed all Lenox china. A Tiffany's executive recalls, "Lenox china was so popular that we still sold it 'under the counter,' but Van would not allow it to be displayed." Truex then set out to visit the English factories of Royal Worcester, Wedgwood, Minton, and Spode. Working closely with Ronald Schwarz, the store's china buyer, he negotiated the revival and redesign of many of the English companies' classic patterns. Under his direction, the craftsmen in each factory adjusted the shapes of individual pieces and refined their colors for the contemporary market. Many of the patterns that he commissioned had not been produced since the beginning of World War I.

Next on his schedule was Paris, where he worked with the renowned French collector and ceramist Camille Le Tallec to produce new china patterns based on eighteenth-century designs. Truex was dissatisfied with the base color of French porcelain, which had a decidedly gray-blue cast; to get around that, and to achieve the classic English shapes he wanted, he had the china produced in England, first by Wedgwood and later by Royal Worcester. The unfinished pieces were sent to Paris to be hand-painted and glazed. Shipping the china first from England to France and then from France to the United States meant that import duty had to be paid twice, which made the final product extremely costly. But despite the exorbitant expense, the venture was another Truex success. Eventually, a French company was able to formulate the base color of porcelain that Truex demanded, and thereafter the china was produced entirely in France. In 1991, Tiffany & Co. would acquire the Le Tallec company, and today, the patterns Truex commissioned—"Coeurs Fleurs," "Directoire," "Les Marronniers," "Bigouden," and "Black Shoulder"—are still sold as Tiffany Private Stock.

From Paris, Truex traveled to Germany, where he commissioned special designs from Nymphenberg Porcelain in Munich and KPM Royal Berlin China in Berlin. The German porcelains were some of the most intricately executed and expensive china patterns ever sold at Tiffany's. Of this group, "Breslau Castle," originally produced for Frederick the Great, was one of the most successful patterns. Truex's own favorite among the German patterns was the elaborate "Nymphenberg." When he elected to create a display that paired this pattern with vermeil flatware, set on a bright-red bandanna-like table cover atop an Oriental rug, he said he was proving to the world that he could work with colors other than beige. His bold use of "Nymphenberg" also emphasized his belief that "china should look like it is made for an individual rather than being based on statistics that supposedly reflect mass taste." The French, German, and English companies that Truex contracted with all agreed that the china produced under his direction would be sold exclusively at Tiffany's. In addition to the manufacturer's mark, each piece would be inscribed, under the glaze, "Made for Tiffany & Co." Truex and Hoving were sensitive to the need to promote the prestige that had long been inherent in the Tiffany hallmark.

Many of the new china patterns and objects that Truex commissioned were the result of research he did at the Metropolitan Museum in New York and the Musée des Arts Décoratifs in Paris. One of the best examples of this is the pattern "Framboise Rose," produced as Tiffany Private Stock. The design gains its richness from a particular pink that was originally used on china made for Empress Elizabeth of Russia by the Imperial Porcelain Manufactory in Saint Petersburg. The prototype on which Truex based "Framboise Rose" remains in the permanent collection of the Metropolitan Museum of Art.

To celebrate the American Bicentennial in 1976, Truex would commission Royal Worcester to reissue, with his modifications, the china pattern originally designed by and for Benjamin Franklin when he served as the first American ambassador to France. When the china arrived at Tiffany's, it was

Wild Strawberry china, Wedgwood, Ltd.

christened "Independence." Truex also worked with Spode to reproduce the china that was used by Thomas Jefferson at Monticello. The unusual character of the pattern was achieved through the application of a cobalt blue spearhead design over a "greystone" body. The unique "greystone" color had been a specialty of the Spode Company since the eighteenth century. Even as he supervised the production of "Monticello," Truex was working on another blue and white pattern based on George Washington's service at Mount Vernon. When the new blue and white patterns were unwrapped at Tiffany's, he proudly pronounced, "They are timeless. Quality is aloof from fashion. Fashion will change, but an article of the right design is good forever."

One of the most successful patterns that Truex introduced was "Wild Strawberry," a design based on an old, almost forgotten pattern originally created by Josiah Wedgwood. John Thomas, who was the director of Wedgwood (USA) when the pattern came on the market, remembers,

> When Van first saw the original Wedgwood strawberry engravings, he envisioned an overall design. Our company designers strongly disagreed with him and said it would never sell. We took his idea and used it as a border, or "shoulder," design. It actually sold quite well, but Van refused to stock the pattern at Tiffany's. Finally, after two years of his insisting, we worked with him to produce an overall strawberry design. This was done against strong advice from our marketing experts. After the design was complete and Van was satisfied, we were determined not to be stuck

with a lot of china we didn't think would sell. To cover ourselves, we said that we would need a minimum order from Tiffany's to put the pattern into production. The "minimum order" we asked for was far in excess of what we would have normally required. When Van heard the number of place settings and service pieces that we were demanding, he said, "Double it." When the china finally arrived in New York, it was an immediate sellout. We couldn't make "Wild Strawberry" fast enough to keep up with the sales. It became our number-one best-selling pattern. In fact, it remains the top pattern at Wedgwood. While it would be impossible to prove, I believe Truex's "Wild Strawberry" is the most successful pattern ever produced by any china maker for the modern market.

One of Truex's most alluring concepts for Tiffany china was his "Floral Armorial" pattern, produced by Minton. The design featured a crest on the shoulder of each plate, but in place of the traditional heraldic emblazonment were festoons of delicate flowers. When the first shipment arrived from England, Truex explained to Elizabeth Franceschini, now a vice president at Tiffany & Co., "I designed 'Floral Armorial' for all the young couples who secretly wish they had an ancestral coat of arms. A happy pasticcio of sorts. On their dining table, it will give a lighthearted semblance of noble lineage."

When Franceschini tells the story of "Floral Amorial," she adds,

Because Van was so exacting, some people thought he was a snob. This was not true. I saw him work with many brides who knew nothing about fine china and did not come from socially elite families. Even if a woman had been reared in an atmosphere of luxury, this did not necessarily mean she was knowledgeable about tableware when she came to Tiffany's to select her first pattern of china and silver. Van was wonderful with these young women. He never made them feel uncomfortable. In fact, just the opposite: he was extremely kind in helping them make their selections. When he was working with a bride, and often the groom was along, Van became the benevolent teacher.

Van dealt with the Tiffany employees in the same way. In the Truex years, we had staff meetings in the morning, before the store opened for customers. At these gatherings, Van informed us about the new merchandise that would be arriving. He always told about how he had designed the things and often gave us the historical background on the designs. The employees looked forward to his lectures. When anyone asked a question—and often the questions were silly—Van would politely listen and give thoughtful, courteous answers. We were all in awe of Van, and quite honestly, everybody loved him.

At no time in his Tiffany years did anything escape Truex's eye as a possible source for a new design. One Monday morning, he came into the store very excited, carrying an eighteenth-century Imari plate that he had borrowed from a lady at whose table he had dined on Saturday evening. He announced that with a few modest changes, the pattern would be perfect for Tiffany's. The ultimate result was "Celestial," a best-seller for the company and Truex's personal pattern of bone china. The introduction of "Celestial" kindled a renewed interest in Japanese design, the original source for many of the wares of Louis Comfort Tiffany. Akin to Truex's mania for food was his fetish for white porcelain, a set of which, he firmly believed, *everyone* should own. To promote that goal, he commissioned Wedgwood to produce, exclusively for Tiffany & Co., a perfectly plain white bone china pattern in classic eighteenth-century shapes. He also had Royal Worcester reissue its eighteenth-century pattern "Blind Earl" in all white.

As Truex grew older, the patterns of china and earthenware he selected for his own use, like everything else in his life, became simpler and more refined. Wedgwood's eighteenth-century faience "Drabware" became his ulti-mate favorite. Extolling its beauty, he said, "Even though Drabware is an awful name, it is the most wonderful color in the world." The color of the faience was derived from a unique gray-brown clay found only in one very small area of England. The color was not painted on; rather, it was inherent in the earth-enware itself. While "Drabware" should have been an inexpensive pattern to produce, it in fact proved extremely costly. The slightest imperfection in the clay, such as a minute iron deposit, would cause discoloration in firing. This uncontrollable quirk of nature produced an extraordinary number of rejects. Because of the high costs involved, "Drabware" was eventually discontinued. Today it is one of the most sought-after and collected of all Tiffany's patterns.

None of Truex's work for Tiffany & Co. was more celebrated than the china he designed for President and Mrs. Lyndon Johnson. When the John-sons moved into the White House, there were not enough place settings of

any single china service for state dinners. Harry Truman had been the last president to have a set of china designed, and the rest was an odd mix-ture of historical pieces (many too valuable to be used) and assorted remnants of sets dat-ing from the Wilson adminis-tration. Truex had actually begun work on a White House commission with Mrs. John F. Kennedy, but the proj-ect was terminated after Presi-dent Kennedy's tragic death.

Truex's Tiffany table setting on a bandanna cover with Nymphen-berg china and silver and vermeil flatware.

Tiffany hostess table setting by Diana Vreeland.

After Lady Bird Johnson decided to commission Tiffany & Co. to make a new set of White House china, Truex's first challenge was to convince President Johnson that there was no company in his native Texas qualified to make the finished product. Once Mrs. Johnson had made it clear that she wanted to break with past formality, insisting that dignity did not have to be either solemn or pompous, the arduous research and work began. After rejecting many conventional designs, she was asked by Truex to consider a pattern based on American wildflowers. Given her interest in landscape beautification, his concept delighted her.

Working from Truex's sketches, André Piette, Tiffany's resident artist, painted the prototype for each piece. The two men achieved a modern look by using the whole plant—flower, stem, and roots—in the style of eighteenth-century botanical prints. Before the china was finally approved, however, the roots were removed. Following tradition and copying the James Monroe china, each service plate was centered with an American eagle. The dinner and dessert plates were designed with different state flowers in the center. It took three years, after the first drawings, to complete the china; the last pieces were not delivered until President Nixon was in office. The 2,190 perfect pieces (250 place settings) were made by Castleton China of Newcastle, Pennsylvania, and cost more than eighty thousand dollars, a sum paid by private donors. Due to the number of people involved in the project, Walter Hoving issued a press release to ensure that there would be no misunderstanding about who was responsible for the finished work. His announcement simply stated, "The White House china for President and Mrs. Johnson was designed by Van Day Truex."

Throughout his years at Tiffany's, Truex would derive enormous satisfaction from designing objects that were elegant but not boringly serious. This side of his nature was most evident in those of his designs that were produced at Este Ceramiche Porcellane in Este, Italy. It was there, working with Count Giovanni Battista Giorgini, that Truex created some of Tiffany's most beautiful faience. When they began working together, in 1955, Giorgini was already famous for his great Italian fashion shows. On one of his frequent trips to the Veneto, he had discovered an old, semiabandoned ceramics works in the town

of Este, not far from Sergio Pizzoni's family estate, Villa Valsanzibio. In the eighteenth century, Este's abundance of a particularly valuable clay, native to the Veneto, had made it the most important ceramics center in Italy.

With their aesthetic sensitivity, Giorgini and Truex both recognized the invaluable design resource to be found in the hundreds of old prints stored in the Este warehouses. Depicting refined forms and elegant dec-

The White House china Truex designed for President and Mrs. Lyndon B. Johnson.

"Frolicking Elephants" table ornaments, commissioned by Truex from the Italian sculptor Andrea Spadini.

orations, the prints were the work of the eighteenth-century masters Jean-Pierre Varion and Gerolamo Franchini. Varion was the French modeler who had first introduced the formula for making porcelain in Italy; the studio that he and Franchini opened in 1780 was to become one of Este's busiest ceramics workshops.

Together, Giorgini and Truex labored to bring Franchini and Varion's work back into production. Inspired by the old designs, the two men produced an enchanting collection of faience that forms a significant chapter in the history of Italian ceramics as well as an important part of the Tiffany tradition. Never relying on mere passive reproduction of previous shapes and styles, they dug deep into their own creativity to design some of the finest services of faience and trompe l'oeil decorative accessories available in the contemporary market. Giorgini's grandson, who now manages the company, proudly keeps a display—almost a small museum—of the objects that his grandfather and Truex created. Many of the pieces that resulted from their collaboration are still in production in Este and are sold not only at Tiffany's but also at Bergdorf Goodman and Nieman Marcus.

One of the most significant examples of Truex's lighthearted approach to design was the collection of porcelain animals he commissioned from the Roman sculptor Andréa Spadini. The white ceramic figurines, produced in sets of six or more figures each, embodied a totally new concept in table decoration. Each set was unique and made without molds so that it could never be reproduced. Truex's ingenious notion of putting these perfectly scaled, baroque yet modern animals on the table was blessed with perfect timing: the elephants, bears, and rhinoceroses arrived at Tiffany's in 1965, just as the Delacorte Clock, also designed by Spadini, was being unveiled in Central Park. The same frolicking animals came out to strike the hour at the children's zoo. The Tiffany Spadini figurines, now collector's items, clearly define Truex's combined sense of elegance and whimsy.

Pierce McGuire, now the head of the Schlumberger Collection at Tiffany's, was an assistant buyer for stationery during the Truex years. He remembers that the creation of the designs for the company Christmas cards caused a major stir and great excitement every April. Hoving always wanted traditional designs, but he also insisted on having something new and different each year. From the first Christmas card meeting until the last, when the designs were finally approved, Hoving was ruthless in his criticism, inevitably resorting to the question "Why doesn't Van come up with some ideas?" And Truex always did. To appease Hoving, he would head for the New York Public Library, the Morgan Library, and the Metropolitan Museum of Art in search of solutions. At each of these institutions, he knew the person to ask for access to ancient manuscripts and prints not seen by the general public. On several occasions, McGuire accompanied him to the private galleries of the museums, where they were shown things that could be handled only by a curator and even then with gloves. Truex would instinctively point to some small detail, such as a tiny bird, a holly leaf, a cherub, or a shepherd, and say, "Use this and only this."

Once, during a particularly heated discussion about the Christmas card designs, Truex took out his pen, drew the outline of three overlapping five-pointed stars, and said, "Print this—one star in copper, one in gold, and one in silver." That year, "The Truex Star," as the design was known, was Tiffany's best-selling Christmas card. According to McGuire, "Everything Van did completely pleased Walter Hoving. Even the Christmas card designs he commissioned from Andy Warhol delighted Hoving. And you must remember, Hoving hated anything that smacked of trendy design."

When Hoving decided that the stationery department should sell Tiffany playing cards, he was his usual demanding self. In meetings with executives from the Bicycle Playing Card Company, he rejected every design they showed him. Finally, Truex was called in. After listening to Hoving's objections to the designs, he sat quietly and sketched a heart, a club, a spade, and a diamond, all in a straight line. He repeated the design over and over until it formed a delicate border around the edge of the card, leaving the center open for the addition of a personal monogram. Farnham Lefferts, then the president of Tiffany's, says, "After weeks of seeing designs and having Hoving reject them all, that morning we sat somewhat spellbound and watched Truex work. Everyone was delighted with his design." Lefferts also remembers the comment made by Bicycle's head designer: "Those hearts, clubs, diamonds, and spades have been with us since the first set of playing cards was printed, but no one has ever used them as beautifully as Truex did today." The design still appears on Tiffany playing cards.

When Hoving bought Tiffany's, in the early 1950s, the company's sterling silver flatware patterns were already American classics. "English King," "Rat Tail," "Olympia," "Audubon," "Shell and Thread," "Fanueil," "Hampton," and "Hamilton" had all been used on elite tables for generations. Hoving, with his usual spirit of innovation, wanted something new. Truex was given the job of designing Tiffany's newest silver pattern. Following in the tradition of Louis Comfort Tiffany, whose designs were taken from natural forms, Truex created "Bamboo." The new flatware was such a success that he soon adapted the design for candlesticks, service plates, and bowls. In 1960, President and Mrs. Eisenhower would present a table centerpiece of four

"Bamboo" candlesticks with a matching bowl to President and Mme. Charles de Gaulle, and in 1966, the pattern would win the International Design Award from the American Institute of Interior Designers.

Over and over, Truex decreed, "In design, Mother Nature is our best teacher." He also believed that "every designer should take himself to the Museum of Natural History and look at the bugs, butterflies, and shells for inspiration." Taking his own advice, he used Karl Blossfeldt's photograph of the fruit *blumenbachia hieronymi,* a rare Argentinean loasa, as the basis for the "Seed Pod" silver centerpiece he designed for Tiffany's. A pair of these centerpieces were presented by President and Mrs. Eisenhower to the king and queen of Thailand on their state visit to the United States in April 1960.

Working with Portugese, Italian, and Mexican craftsmen, Truex designed many other pieces of silver that were unique to Tiffany & Co. One of his personal favorites, which also sold extremely well, was a serving basket for fruit or bread, woven in sterling silver. Another favorite was his silver Strawberry Box, based on the small wooden boxes used in the market for berries.

Two of his most celebrated designs were the palm tree candlesticks and monkey candle holders that he modeled after eighteenth-century originals in the Musée de Carnavalet. Both of these, as well as his Strawberry Box, were also produced in vermeil. When John Pierrepont saw the vermeil pieces, his response was, "Van, everything you touch turns to gold."

Four sterling containers commissioned by Truex for Tiffany & Co. The seed pod on the far left is taken from a photograph by Karl Blossfeldt.

An assortment of Truex designs produced for Tiffany & Co.: Blossfeldt seedpod, Baccarat "Dionysus" decanter, "Rock Crystal" candlesticks, carriage clock, "Bamboo" flatware, and "Framboise Rose," Tiffany Private Stock porcelain.

While some of the things that Truex designed were comparatively inexpensive, many others were well beyond the price range of most Tiffany customers. La Bar Hoagland, Tiffany's executive vice president, said "There is a certain amount of stuff that we put out there that will never sell well, but it creates an atmosphere that enables us to sell a hell of a lot of other stuff." Working closely with the designers at Brierly Crystal, Ltd., in England, Truex adapted the antique "Swag" crystal pattern to create a new version that would become a Tiffany classic. By eliminating the original's ornate and elaborate cutting, he produced a pattern that is reminiscent of art deco but evinces its own timeless, modern character. Another of Truex's original patterns was "Rock Crystal," which, like "Swag," is still produced in myriad forms and is available in a wide variety of shapes.

In the 1960s, Truex accepted a commission from Baccarat to design a line of crystal that would be sold exclusively at Baccarat and Tiffany & Co. One of the many pieces to come out of this commission was his "Dionysus" decanter. In 1978, the Architecture and Design Committee of the Museum of Modern Art would select the "Dionysus" decanter for the museum's Permanent Design Collection. Truex himself always referred to the decanter as his "Van Ordinaire Carafe"; when he gave one as a gift, he would include a simple cork, saying that he much preferred the natural material to the crystal stopper he had designed for it.

Truex's other "outside" commissions during his Tiffany years came from two New York firms, Hinson & Co. and the Edward Fields Carpet Company. Harry Hinson commissioned him to design a small chair that could be easily moved from one seating group to another during a cocktail party. Hinson described what he had in mind as a "pull-up" chair. The small black wooden chair that Truex designed for him has a padded seat that is slightly lower than typical seating height, and a curved back carved in such a way that the upper section forms a handle for portability. While the delicate lines of the

Collection of crystal designed for Tiffany & Co., including far left, "Rock Crystal" candlestick and, far right, "All-Purpose" wineglass.

finished chair recall the furniture produced in France during the reign of Napoleon III, the overall simplicity of its design makes it suitable for both traditional and modern rooms. The carpet Truex designed for Edward Fields was the direct result of a decorating commission from Mr. and Mrs. Vincent Astor. According to Edward Fields, Jr., Truex contacted his father with a request for "dogproof" carpeting—something, he specified, that would not show the stains left by Mr. Astor's three Great Danes and his miniature Mexican burro, all of which were allowed to wander freely in the Astors' library. Mr. Fields told him that his company offered no such design and suggested that Truex come up with something himself. In response, Truex produced a design in dark earth-tone colors, for either wall-to-wall wool carpeting or area rugs, incorporating overlapping patterns that resemble animal skins. The carpet, which he named "Terra," met the Astors' needs perfectly. It became a classic in the Edward Fields, Inc., inventory and is still produced today in many color combinations.

From his earliest days at the R. H. Macy Company, Hoving had always been driven by a passionate concern for good design. Being a well-educated man, a graduate of Brown University, he wanted to know as much as possible about art history and antiques. During his Macy's years, he took evening courses three nights a week at the Metropolitan Museum of Art, where he studied antique furniture, textiles, carpets, silver, and china. These courses formed the foundation for Hoving's thesis "Good Design Is Good Business."

In 1975, Hoving would work with the Wharton School of Business to produce the Tiffany-Wharton Lectures on Corporate Design Management. The speakers for the series were Louis I. Kahn, Edgar Kaufmann, Thomas J. Watson, Jr., George O'Brien, Hoving, and Truex. The lectures were given at the Wharton School in Philadelphia and published under the title *The Art of Design Management.* In his introduction to the book, Tom Schutte refers to Walter Hoving as "the business community's Jeremiah of good design." The series was well received throughout the American corporate business community, and in 1976, the English fabric manufacturer Clarence House gave copies of the book to all of its top customers. In his lecture, "The Environment for Creating Good Design," Truex emphasized that "Training the eye is the most important way to gain an appreciation and understanding of good design in business management." His work at Tiffany's, and his close personal relationship with Hoving, had given him the confidence to set forth a mandate: "Management must abandon its primary orientation of 'Will it sell?' and ask the more basic question, 'How is the product to look?' "

After seven exciting but ex-

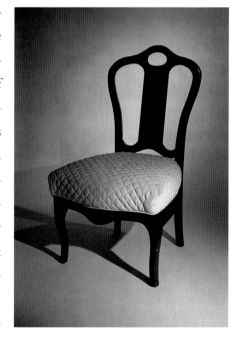

Truex chair, commissioned by Harry Hinson & Company, New York.

hausting years of working with Hoving, Truex was acutely aware that he had never used Mona Bismarck's gift to buy a house. He had been too busy to think about anything but his work and the success of Tiffany & Co. While he had been to Europe innumerable times, it had always been on company business, and his schedule had left him little time to look for real estate. Since his first visit to the south of France, in 1930, he had never lost his yearning to live in Provence, the land of Bonnard, Cézanne, and Matisse. He had kept numerous photographs of his excursions with the Garretts to Aix, Arles, Saint-Rémy, Avignon, Marseilles, and many of the smaller villages that gave that part of France its character. To his mind, it was in this region, where the cultures of Italy, Spain, and the ancient East melded, that the essence of French culture had been formed. In 1962, Truex finally bought a house, in the ancient fortress town of Gordes. When he announced, four years later, that he wanted to be in France for a greater portion of each year, Hoving consented, but only on the condition that he stay on as a special consultant and find someone to be his successor.

In 1967, Truex recommended that Hoving hire his friend George O'Brien as Tiffany's new director of design. Twenty-three years younger than Truex and a graduate of the University of California at Berkeley, O'Brien had an intellectual bent and a keen interest in modern design. The biography of him in the Tiffany archives states that he had "written articles for everything from *Sports Illustrated* to *Art in America* and . . . published *The New York Times Book of Design and Decoration*. After graduating from Berkeley, he . . . worked in the publications department of the Museum of Modern Art. From then on he worked on various home furnishing publications which included being an assistant editor of Home Living at *Look,* editor of Home News for the *New York Times,* and feature editor of *Home Furnishings Daily,* among others." According to one of Tiffany's retired senior executives, "The 'among others' was Hoving's deft omission of the fact that when O'Brien was hired, he was the

Modern Living editor at *Playboy*. The very mention of such a publication could bode friction with Hoving. The idea of *Playboy* magazine was the kind of thing that set Walter's teeth on edge." Whatever reservations Hoving may have had, on Truex's recommendation, he hired O'Brien as vice president and director of design.

When O'Brien started at Tiffany's, Hoving was having to face the reality that the charmed 1950s, the Eisenhower years, were over. A new age, the 1960s, was in place. It was a time marked by the turbulence of the Vietnam War, the emergence of the hippie culture, and the omnipresence of a young populace that showed a blatant disregard for conventional social mores. Walter Hoving was frustrated by what was happening in the world around him, and he despised the home furnishings and accessories that emerged in this era. Many of the ideas being generated were in direct opposition to his traditional taste. O'Brien, by contrast, had an understanding and appreciation of the new art and design. The best example of his forward thinking was his recognition of Elsa Peretti's talent: it was a major achievement for Tiffany's when he persuaded Hoving to acquire the exclusive rights to her work. But even the success of Peretti's designs did not convince Hoving. Each year, when Truex returned from France, Hoving would be waiting for the opinions of his former, trusted design director.

Hoving's disillusionment with the culture led him enthusiastically to embrace an evangelical spirit of Christianity. He even designed a piece of silver jewelry, intended to be worn as a tie tack or lapel pin, that said, "Try God." O'Brien vividly remembers that when he refused to wear one of the "Try God" pins, Hoving accused him of being an "atheistic Catholic." O'Brien defended himself by saying that he thought religion was a private matter, adding that while he had been reared a Catholic, he no longer attended church. Hoving angrily responded, "But you're still an atheist." The situation would grow more and more intolerable until, in 1978, O'Brien's relationship with the company came to an end. Letitia Baldrige, who had been the public-relations director for Tiffany's and was well acquainted with the charmed partnership of Hoving and Truex, said, "No matter who Walter [had] hired when Van left, it would not have worked. He had a unique working relationship with Van, and he wasn't going to be happy with anyone [else]."

With O'Brien out of the company, Hoving immediately called Truex in France and insisted that he return to Tiffany's. His proposal included a vice presidency, with a substantial salary and all company benefits. His only requirement was that Truex remain in New York City until a new design director could be hired. He said the official word in the company was that George O'Brien was "opening his own consulting firm." People close to the situation, including Truex himself, were aware that O'Brien had left under extremely strained circumstances. Truex also knew that O'Brien held him partially responsible for the events that had led to his departure. As far as Truex was concerned, their friendship had begun unraveling six years before, after he bought a house in Bedford, New York, to use when he was not in Provence. To cover the expense of owning two houses, one in France and the other in the United States, he had proposed that O'Brien rent the Bedford house and commute to Tiffany's in New York City. The arrangement had lasted less than a year; from the beginning, the two men had disagreed about financial responsibilities, the use of space, and personal privileges. When they were unable to resolve their differences, O'Brien had moved back to the city. Without his rent, Truex had been forced to sell the house. The whole debacle had been a blow to his pride.

On leaving Bedford, O'Brien had moved into the Beekman Townhouse, an apartment building on the corner of Third Avenue and East Sixty-third Street. Truex, meanwhile, still needing a base in New York, had moved into a Park Avenue apartment owned by a friend, only to be informed that the friend had decided to sell the place. He had then leased the apartment directly above O'Brien's in the Beekman Townhouse. This proximity had served only to hasten the demise of their friendship. As to what had happened between O'Brien and Hoving—well, Truex stoically believed that unpleasant occurrences were a part life, especially in the business world. He remembered how it had been when he faced a similar situation at Parsons in 1952. Then, he had marshaled his innner strength and discipline and moved on to a new career. To his mind, any person of character and resolve could do the same thing.

The news of George O'Brien's departure spread quickly through the New York design community, but speculation over who would replace him at Tiffany & Co. was short-lived. When Eleanor Lambert, one of Hoving's and Truex's most trusted friends, called and recommended John Loring for the job, the die was cast. Loring, who was then working for Paige Rense at *Architectural Digest,* met all of Hoving's requirements for the job: he had gone to Yale and studied at the Ecole des Beaux Arts, was fluent in French, had lived in Europe, and was socially well connected. One executive at Tiffany's remembers that when Loring joined the company, Hoving, in his new spirit of Christian evangelism, went around the store quoting from the Bible, "There was a man sent by God whose name was John."

Three Houses in the South of France

*I*n the spring of 1930, John and Alice Garrett had invited Truex to join them for a motor trip through Provence. During their three weeks together, they had visited Avignon, Aix, Saint-Rémy, Arles, and several villages in the Lubéron Valley. The ancient cities and rugged countryside had made an indelible impression on Truex. Writing about the Lubéron Valley in *Architectural Digest* in 1975, Truex said, "The countryside is strong and lovely, with a bracing climate of sun and wind. A mixture of dramatic elements of nature and a careful cultivation, the land is rich with ancient history: Celtic, Greek, Roman. There are innumerable historical sites to be found: ruins, old hilltop villages, architectural remains of ancient convents, castles, fortresses. It seems that almost every day there is some new and fascinating site to be discovered, and this largess has given the residents of this part of Provence a certain sense of local pride." His dream of living in this valley, which began on his first visit, had become a reality in 1962.

When Truex first saw the magnificent front doors of the Louis XIII–period house in the ancient fortress town of Gordes, in 1962, he knew that this was where he wanted to live. Not only did he love the house; he was enchanted, too, by the village, which he described as an "almost perfect hillside community." After buying the property, he quickly became a part of the community and was well received by the local citizens, who were both de-

Entrance to the house in Gordes, Provence.

Gordes, Provence.

lighted and amused by the co-ordinated beige outfits he wore. The village baker, who worked in his grandfather's bake shop when Truex lived in Gordes, remembers, "Monsieur Truex was always immaculately dressed, even in the early-morning hours when he walked down the hill for his baguette. He was never without a jacket. Our other customers, at that hour, looked as if they had just gotten out of bed. Monsieur Truex was different." The baker was not alone in his admiration of his customer's sartorial elegance. In 1974, Truex would be inducted into the International Hall of Fame as one of the best-dressed men in the world.

The fact that the house in Gordes had been owned by André Lhote, the surrealist painter, only added to Truex's fascination with the ancient structure. With its massive staircase in the entrance, the grand proportions of its gallery, and its spacious private rooms, the place had every architectural component he had dreamed of. He was also pleased that Lhote had never really renovated the house. This would allow him to do his own restoration without having to alter the previous owner's mistakes.

The house was located on the eastern side of Gordes, and every window on the southern exposure provided a dramatic view of the Lubéron Valley. Throughout the house, there were exceptional fireplaces and overmantels and remarkable stone details. The one bath and one toilet were serviced by outmoded plumbing and had crude old-fashioned fixtures. The kitchen was barely adequate. The ancient terraces were crumbling and in great need of repair. But the purchase price of the house and the estimated costs of renovation were within the budget Truex had set for the project. He felt confident that with Mona Bismarck's gift and his other savings, he had more than enough money for the things he wanted to accomplish.

Having never actually done any renovating himself, Truex was completely unaware that construction expenses on an old house could run to twice the estimated cost, and usually did. The two biggest expenditures that he did not figure into his budget were a new roof and the support structures that were needed for the terraces. Nor did he account for the extraordinary expenditure that would be required to meet the specifications imposed by the

Interior of the grand salon of the house in Gordes, Provence.

Bâtiments de France Administrative on the restoration of every historic building. These rigid regulations applied to both interior and exterior renovations.

In making plans for the restoration, Truex felt strongly that he wanted
to work personally with the local artisans and craftsmen, and thus he elected
not to hire an architect or general contractor. From the first day of construction, when work began on the foundations and outside walls, to the last, when
Truex suffered the frustration of matching the color of existing stonework,
the costs were phenomenal. The addition of electricity, plumbing, and proper
drainage brought expenses that quickly went far beyond his budget. The regulations governing the restoration of historic buildings stipulated that roof re-
pairs could not be done on exterior tiles, so the roofers had to work from
inside the roof structure—one more nightmare and outpouring of money. If
any exterior tiles had to be replaced, only antique tiles could be used. The
coup de grâce was the work on the terraces. Not one of the original retaining
walls of the gardens was sound, and to keep the house from falling off the side
of the mountain, new support structures had to be built at every level. It was
just as well that Truex was committed to the idea of minimal furnishings and
had never intended to have expensive furniture or antiques, because it was
clear that by the time construction was completed, he would have virtually no
money left. The real problem, he realized, was that in order to maintain the
house properly after the work was finished, he would need a full-time staff,
including a gardener. The house of his dreams had become his worst nightmare.

Everyone in Gordes was impressed with the work Truex had done and
sympathetic about his economic plight. The financial officer with whom he
dealt at the local bank advised him to sell the place immediately and invest in
a more modest property. As awful as that idea sounded to him, he knew he
could not afford to keep the house. He put word out that he was willing to sell
it at a price that would enable him to recoup his investment. The fact that the

final details were still unfinished would, he thought, be an advantage, as it would allow a new owner to make any last modifications he or she wished. Once again, Truex's customary luck would prevail.

Barry Sainsbury, a London antiques dealer, and his wife, Cynthia, were just then visiting Truex's friend Daniel Kiener in the neighboring village of Joucas. Like most people who came to the Lubéron Valley, the young couple fell in love with the rustic charm of the region. When Sainsbury announced that he would like to buy some property, Kiener told him that Truex's house was for sale. That evening, Sainsbury called Truex and asked if he might come for a visit. The following morning, after seeing the work that had been done on the house, he agreed to pay its owner's asking price. Sainsbury would eventually carry out all of Truex's original plans, add a swimming pool, and furnish the house with antiques appropriate to its majesty. Five years later, when

everything was completed, the house would be featured in the *New York Times Magazine*. Although he had not finished the project, Truex had learned that achieving simplicity and suitability was not necessarily a low-cost proposition.

Truex would derive his greatest joy from the experience in 1967, when the Queen Mother of England, traveling with Charles de Noailles, visited Barry and Cynthia Sainsbury. At a luncheon party given in her honor, the Queen

H. M. Queen Elizabeth of England, the Queen Mother, on a visit to Gordes, Provence, 1967. Cynthia Sainsbury, with back to camera, and Charles de Noailles.

Mother would inform Truex that the Sainsburys had credited him with the original designs for the restoration. She complimented him on his vision and said that she thought he had done "a masterful job of restoring the soul of an important building, adding to the culture of France." The pleasure he took in her approval was enhanced by the fact that the two of them were old friends. He had often dined with her or taken tea in her home when visiting Burnet Pavitt and John Mallet at Bury Farm, the small house they leased on her Bowes Lyon family estate in Hertfordshire.

After the Sainsburys bought the place in Gordes and Truex moved to his next house, near a neighboring town, the three of them would become quite close. He met and befriended many of their English visitors, among them David and Pamela Hicks, whose company he greatly enjoyed. When he was first introduced to them, Hicks was just launching his career in interior decorating. Truex was impressed with the young designer's talent and arranged for him to meet Billy Baldwin in New York City; Baldwin in turn introduced him to the leading New York decorators and the most important home-furnishing designers in America. Hicks would later tell Barry Sainsbury that Truex and Baldwin had shaped many of the concepts that established him as one of England's leading decorators.

Having narrowly escaped financial disaster in Gordes, Truex began searching for a less costly house. Determined to live in the valley between the Vaucluse and the Lubéron Mountains, Truex in 1964 bought an abandoned farmhouse that he named Chaumet ("thatched cottage"), on twenty acres of rugged land outside the town of Gargas. Chaumet was in far worse structural condition than the house in Gordes had been, but it was much smaller. The rural location was outside the jurisdiction of the Bâtiments de France Admin-istrative, which meant that he could make the necessary adaptations on a much smaller budget. This is not to suggest that he was any less sensitive to the landscape and local architecture when he restored Chaumet; indeed, he did

Living room, Chaumet, Gargas, Provence.

everything he could to ensure that the house was in keeping with its sur-roundings. Again choosing not to hire an architect, Truex planned the renova-tions and then, working with local craftsmen, supervised the entire reconstruction. But when Chaumet was finished, he found that it was not really what he wanted. Looking back on it later, he would say, "The whole experience was far too much work. The house was so isolated that no one wanted to come for dinner for fear of getting lost. It was hell." During the five years that Truex lived in Chaumet, he would come to realize that he was a person who needed a community. While he was comfortable living alone, he

Living-room fireplace,
Chaumet, Gargas,
Provence.

also enjoyed the company of others, and in Gargas, there were days when he saw no one unless he drove to a neighboring town. To ward off loneliness, he acquired his first and only pet, a stray cat. Having described the Chaumet experience as "hell," he aptly named the cat Diablo.

In spite of the frustrations and isolation of Gargas, Truex's work on Chaumet was a triumph. Not only did he succeed in his quest for simplicity in the renovation and furnishing of the house; he also learned to use native plants and ground cover in his landscaping. Everyone he invited to Chaumet was enthusiastic about his accomplishments. In May 1968, Georges and Rosamund Bernier ran a feature article on Chaumet in their magazine, *L'Œil,* and they also included a chapter on the house in their book *European Decoration: Creative Contemporary Interiors.* The following August, 1969, just before he sold the house, the *New York Times Magazine* published a feature juxtaposing Chaumet with Truex's Park Avenue apartment. The double focus of the article, rural France coupled with New York City, stressed Truex's passion for natural materials in decorating and his use of straw, cotton, animal prints, and, above all, the color beige.

All that Truex had learned from renovating two old houses now sparked his ambition to create a completely new house. He had had enough of

Truex's bedroom, Chaumet, Gargas, Provence.

the compromises required in installing plumbing and modern conveniences in ancient buildings. In 1969, after much wrangling with the local authorities, Truex finally purchased a small strip of land on the edge of a mountain in Ménerbes. The village, dating from the sixteenth century, was built along the top of a narrow, wooded hill below the northern slopes of the Lubéron. Whereas other Provençal hill villages differ in character between their lower and upper halves, Ménerbes is an elongated community, with the principal division being between its western and eastern sides. The western, where Truex's house was located, is the livelier of the two: it contains the village café, bakery, meat market, and general store and is the site of the weekly street market. In recent years, owing to the popularity of the book *A Year in Provence,* by the English advertising executive Peter Mayle, Ménerbes has become a tourist mecca, but when Truex bought his property, it was still a quiet country hamlet.

While searching for a lot on which to build, Truex met Henri-Alex André Favre, a young architect who was a native of Provence. Fascinated by Truex's sense of style and his knowledge of French architecture and the decorative arts, Favre agreed to work with him on his house. Friends who were close to the project recall, "Van designed the house; Favre did the drafting." When Truex was working on the designs, nothing was left to chance, and every detail was planned for total simplicity and comfort.

Dining terrace, Chaumet, Gargas, Provence.

Having learned his lesson in restoring the terraces in Gordes, Truex commissioned a topographical survey of the Ménerbes property. The site he had chosen for the foundation of the house was deemed safe for building, but he was cautioned about the limestone hill in back: the engineer who did the survey said the limestone might hold for centuries, as it had already done, or it might come crashing down on the house at any time. Truex decided to take the gamble. This time, he was determined to

have exactly the house he had always wanted. After owning the
Gordes and Gargas houses, he was
clear about the ideal proportions
for the rooms and the requirements for his own comfort. He
definitely did not want an extensive garden. He did want a living
room large enough to serve as a
dining room; a small but efficient
kitchen; and two guest rooms,
each with its own bath and toilet.
He wanted his own bedroom,
bathroom, and toilet to be located
well away from the guest rooms.
For the kitchen and baths, he
specified white porcelain fixtures
with simple chrome and stainless
steel fittings. Since the day he first
saw the nautilus-chamber stairway that Le Corbusier had de-

signed in 1930 for Charles de Beistegui's Paris apartment, he had dreamed of *Nautilus staircase,* having one just like it. The nautilus stairway now became the center of his in- *Ménerbes, Provence.* terior plan.

The exterior and interior walls of the house were to be finished in the same texture; the color, if any, would be added to the plaster before it was ap-plied. Truex wanted no paint on any of the wall surfaces. The door and win-dow lintels were to be cut from native stone, with no superfluous detail. The floors would be natural-color glazed terra cotta tiles made by local potters. All

*Living room,
Ménerbes, Provence.*

of the teakwood trim of the interior and exterior was to be left in its natural state, with no paint, stain, or varnish applied. For the draperies, Truex intended to use the same sturdy cotton he had hung in Gargas.

By the time the house was ready for him to move into, Truex had acquired all the furniture and accessories he would need. The rattan and wooden furniture had all been made locally. He had two sets of dishes—one all white, the other a bright saffron yellow made from the indigenous clay of the neighboring village of Roussillon. The lamps were fashioned out of large aubergine wine bottles of the sort used by local wineries. All of the bed and bath linens were white, and the table linens were either natural linen or chocolate brown.

The only decorative objects in the house were a few pieces of primitive African art, some trompe l'oeil plates from the collection he had designed in Este for Tiffany's, and his own paintings. The overall effect was of order and simplicity. Truex had achieved all he wanted and more—which for him meant less.

Remembering his first visit to the Ménerbes house, Hubert de Givenchy would say, "I admired everything that Van had done. The house was, first of all, an honest house. Extremely modest, it had a monastic quality. The bare-bone details embodied style and sophistication. It was so remarkably pure that it made me want to go home and eliminate the unnecessary things from my own house. If I had to think of one word to describe Van's taste, I would say it was *cashmere*. The finest and rarest cashmere. Being in the fashion business, I offer this as my highest praise."

Truex's housekeeper, Merielle Birolini, lived across the street from the entrance to his driveway, and his American artist friends Jane Eakin and Joe Downing each had a house only a short distance from his front door. Although he was never close to either Eakin or Downing, both were dependable neighbors. For Truex, this meant that they were there if he needed anything, and in like fashion, he was there for them, but this assurance did not necessitate an intimate social relationship. His only close friend in the Lubéron was Rory Cameron.

From the day he met Cameron, Truex had been fascinated by the younger man's knowledge of the decorative arts. Cameron not only had a natural gift for decorating but also possessed the refinement and taste that come from always being exposed to the best of everything. When they were introduced, in the early 1950s, Cameron was living with his mother, the Countess of Kenmare, at Villa La Fiorentina at Saint-Jean-Cap-Ferrat. La Fiorentina was then, and still is, regarded as the most beautiful villa on the Côte d'Azur.

Enid Kenmare was a celebrated beauty who had left her native Australia at a young age and subsequently married three times. Each of her husbands was reported to have been among the richest men in the world. Her first husband, Cameron's father, had been an American of Scottish descent. Soon after his death, when Cameron was a small child, Enid had married Lord Cavendish, with whom she had had two more children. Cavendish, like her third husband, Lord Kenmare, was English. Rory and his two half-siblings, the Honorable Patricia O'Neill and Lord Caryll Waterpark, had been educated in French, Egyptian, English, Swiss, and German schools.

When Cameron was still a child, his mother had skillfully directed his exposure to the arts. He had never bothered to acquire a university education but instead had taken advantage of the opportunity afforded him by Enid's great wealth to travel the world and explore the capitals of Europe. Cameron would write nine books about his life and travels, including *The Golden Riviera,* a history of Provence and an account of his time on the Côte d'Azur.

Along with Cameron's other myriad friends, Truex had been a frequent visitor at Villa La Fiorentina in the 1950s. It was there that he had met Walter Lees, who in time would become one of his closest confidants. When they were introduced, Lees was already well established in his career in public relations. He would later become a much-celebrated international photographer. Charles Sevigny, one of Truex's former students, and Yves Vidal, the director of the European offices of Knoll International, were also often at La Fiorentina in those years. Following Sevigny's graduation from Parsons, just after World War II, Truex had been instrumental in getting him his first job, decorating and refurbishing the American embassies in Europe for the U.S. State Department. Sevigny had subsequently gone on to become one of the most celebrated interior designers in France.

In 1961, Cameron had sold La Fiorentina to an American couple, Mr. and Mrs. Harding Lawrence, and moved to the neighboring dower house, Le Clos, where he and his mother had lived during their extensive restoration of the villa. As the Riviera became more and more crowded, Cameron yearned for a quieter life. Finally, in 1965, he sold Le Clos to Hubert de Givenchy and moved to Ireland, where he bought a house near his friends Henry McIlhenny and Derek Hill. McIlhenny, a wealthy American, owned a formidable estate named Castle Glengeagh, and Hill, the noted English painter, was close by in the historically significant Glebe House (now an Irish National Trust museum). Unfortunately for Cameron, however, Hill spent most of his time in London, and McIlhenny, who lived in Philadelphia, was at Castle Glengeagh only infrequently. When his two friends were away, County Donegal proved to be a lonely place for Rory Cameron.

In 1971, on one of his many visits to Cameron's Irish estate, Truex enticed him to move to the Lubéron Valley and build a house. It took little persuasion to get Cameron out of Ireland and back to France: though he was by birth an American citizen, France had become his home. Following Truex's design, Cameron broke ground for Les Quatre Sources in the valley between the villages of Ménerbes and Les Baumettes. Almost as soon as it was completed, Les Quatre Sources became a much-photographed and much-publicized house. Its location on a hillside facing Ménerbes, the oversized scale of its rooms (an unusual feature in Provençal architecture), and its remarkable staircase were all Truex's designs. While Truex himself thought his house in Ménerbes was his finest work, since the discovery of his original plans for Cameron's house, in 1987, most designers have considered Les Quatre Sources his masterpiece.

Marguerite Littman, a friend of Barry and Cynthia Sainsbury's, frequently visited both Truex and Cameron. In 1974, she wrote articles for *House and Garden* about each of them and her visits to their houses in the Lubéron. Her story on Truex, focusing on his house and his innate flair for entertaining, recounts a luncheon he gave for her and their shared friends Stephen and Natasha Spender, who lived in the neighboring village of Saint-Rémy-de-

Truex photograph of Marguerite Littman, left, with Rosamund Bernier, taken at Kitty Miller's home in Mallorca.

Provence. To emphasize Truex's passion for cooking, Littman included his recipes for Green Chicken, for his version of the traditional Provençal daube, and for one of his staple desserts, a compote of stewed fruits. Her two articles confirm that Truex and Cameron were both excellent cooks, a trait that, when combined with their common understanding of hospitality, elegance, and simplicity, abetted their close friendship. Mrs. William McCormick Blair, the acknowledged arbiter of taste in the city of Washington, who was also a frequent houseguest of both Truex's and Cameron's, said, "I will always remember Van [as] having the most rare and beautiful imagination of any man I ever met. His impact on the decorative arts was not ever, in any way or sense, wild or extravagant but always restrained, disciplined, and transforming."

In 1969, when he was sixty-five years old, Truex moved to Ménerbes. That same year, he was notified that his sister Phyllis had died. Fifteen years earlier, in 1954, the same year that his mother died, his younger sister, Mary, had died in an institution for disabled persons. Ten years later, in 1964, his father, then ninety-six, had died in Indio, California. In his scrapbooks, Truex kept two snapshots, both dated 1939, of his siblings. One is of his sisters, Phyllis and Mary, photographed at Aunt Kee's summer home, Yap Kanum, in Wisconsin. The other is of his younger brother, Herbert, who would have been twenty-nine when the picture was taken. In the photo, Herbert is quite handsome and nattily dressed, leaning against an open convertible coupe. Truex kept no pictures of his parents; the two photographs of his siblings were his only records or mementos of his past. Now, in 1972, he received a letter from Herbert's wife, Eleanor, informing him that his brother, after a long battle with alcoholism, had taken his own life. Truex, at sixty-eight, was the last surviving member of his immediate family.

John Mallet and Burnet Pavitt were visiting him when the news of Herbert's death came. Pavitt remembers, "It was one of the few times I ever saw Van show any emotion. He talked about being without any family and the fact that he had no one close to him. While I was sympathetic, as one always is in such situations, I remember thinking that it would have been impossible for Van to ever share his life with anyone. I had known him since he first came to Paris, as a student, in 1925. He simply wasn't the kind of person who could have a partner." Reflecting Pavitt's sentiments, Joe Downing says, "It would have never worked for Van to have someone in his life. He was driven by his search for perfection. This kind of compulsion does not allow room for sharing your life. While I liked Van very much, I don't think anyone could have folded a napkin to suit him."

Daniel Kiener, the friend who had sent Barry Sainsbury to Gordes, concurred but also recalled a very different side of Truex: "When I knew Van in Provence, he always seemed totally absorbed in his painting. He was absolutely obsessed with perfection. There was a time when I thought his 'minimalist' behavior, which everyone who knew him talked about, was a nice way of saying he was stingy. But I was wrong. I remember that when my son died, on the day of the funeral, in our confused state, we had forgotten to order flowers for the grave. Just as the service was starting, Van arrived with four enormous pots of white roses. He had an innate sense of doing the right thing and doing it beautifully."

Approaching his seventieth birthday, Truex nurtured his closest friends, who often came for extended visits. Walter Lees, Burnet Pavitt and John Mallet, and the Laurance Robertses were his most frequent visitors. Whenever he had guests, Truex maintained strict rules about mealtimes, daily activities, and schedules for getting up in the morning and retiring at night. Bedtime was ten-thirty for everyone in the house. Women guests were asked to arrange their next day's breakfast tray each evening; the following morning, promptly at eight o'clock, Truex would delivered the tray to their bedroom door. Men were expected to come downstairs—fully dressed, never in a robe—for all meals. Breakfast always consisted of fruit and fresh bread that Truex had purchased before his guests awoke; often he drove to Cavaillon before dawn and

Walter Lees, left, *with Truex in Provence.*

shopped for produce at the open market. At nine o'clock, the maid came to clean the kitchen and tidy the bedrooms. If Truex was having a dinner party, she would stay into the afternoon and help with the preparations.

Truex's lifelong obsession with modest servings of food provided a reliable source of good-natured humor for his friends. Isabel Roberts recalls, "Van maintained a very strict rule about drinking. Guests were allowed one cocktail before dinner but never two. If he invited four people for dinner, the meal he served would have barely fed three." She conceded, however, that "while his meals were always delicious, food per se was never the point. With Van, style was what ultimately mattered. He set the most beautiful table in the world and entertained with unsurpassed elegance." Her sentiments were shared by most, if not all, of his friends. Hubert de Givenchy remembers being shocked at the evening meal Truex served when he and Mrs. Paul Mellon paid a visit to Ménerbes: "I did expect that for Mrs. Mellon he might have had a chicken or a small chop. Instead we were served soup, bread, and some fruit. That was it. As I look back on the experience, I realize that it was Van's way of maintaining his individual style. Total simplicity. But all so very elegantly presented."

When Truex had guests, he chauffeured them on day trips to the neighboring towns of Gordes, Roussillon, Bonnieux, Saint-Rémy, Arles, Aix-en-Provence, and Avignon. Proud of the Lubéron Valley, he took great pleasure in being the resident tour guide. He and his guests were regularly asked to lunch and dinner with friends, but Truex always preferred eating at home. An invitation to dine with Rory Cameron was the one exception he happily made.

Hiély-Lucullus in Avignon and Rose d'Or in Roussillon were the only local restaurants that Truex enjoyed. He and Cameron ate at Hiély at least once a week and thought of it as "almost like being at home." Over time, Hiély's

owner would become one of Truex's close Provençal friends. He commissioned Truex to decorate the restaurant, purchased four of his large paintings to
hang in the entranceway, and reproduced another of his works on the cover of
Hiély's menu. Even though the original owner of the restaurant died some
years ago, the new proprietor has not changed either the decor or the menu
cover, and Truex's paintings remain today the focal point of the restaurant.

Truex had always believed that "The best friend a single man can have
is an older woman with taste and style. It is more convenient if the woman is
divorced or a widow." Certainly he had had his share of such friends, and unquestionably each one had played a dramatic role in his life and career.
Through these women, he had come to know some of the most important
people in the world. For all the social success he had achieved, however, it
bothered him to think that he had entered the world of power and privilege
on somebody else's coattail. He confessed to Laurance Roberts that he was
haunted by the idea that he was accepted in elite circles only because he kept
company with socially prominent, wealthy women. He further told Laurance
that he was sure he could achieve the status he wanted if he became a member
of one of New York's prestigious men's clubs. In such an environment, he felt,
he would be able to mingle with the other members on his own merit. Once
he had received the bad report on his heart condition and knew that he was
returning to New York, he made up his mind that the club for him was the
Knickerbocker. Not only did he consider the Knick (as it is called by members) the top club in the city, but it also offered him some definite advantages.
Located only a few blocks north of Tiffany's, it would be convenient for meals
and entertaining. Confident that admission would not be a problem, before
leaving Ménerbes, he wrote to two close friends who were members and said
he would like to be proposed for membership.

The very day the Ménerbes house went on the market, there was a potential buyer. The initial contracts were signed, and Truex thought he had a sure sale, but then the limestone hill behind the house caved in. Tons of stone crashed within feet of the back side of the house. The buyer withdrew his offer, and Truex was faced with the task of removing the debris and securing the face of the cliff. Fortunately, no damage was done to the house, and as soon as the scree had been cleared away and the landscaping repaired, another buyer appeared. In keeping with Truex's usual good luck, while the work was being done, the value of the French franc rose dramatically, so he ended up realizing a far greater profit from the sale than he would have done if the first contract had gone through. Once the sale was final, he flew to New York City.

Future Plans

When Truex arrived in New York in November 1978, he was relieved to learn that George O'Brien had already vacated his office at Tiffany & Co. and left on an extended vacation. This meant that the two of them would not meet, even by chance, at the apartment building on East Sixty-third Street. But as happy as he was to know that O'Brien was out of town, Truex was equally *un*happy that Billy Baldwin had decided to give up his apartment and move permanently to Nantucket. This news came as no big surprise. Five years before, in 1973, Baldwin had officially retired and sold his business, Baldwin, Martin and Smith, to his partner Arthur Smith. Since then, he had spent most of his time on the island.

Truex was thankful that Albert Hadley, at least, was in New York. Since the day Hadley had first entered Parsons as a student, Truex had held him in the highest esteem. Even though he had been away during much of the period when Hadley was establishing his career in interior decorating, the two men had kept in touch. In 1967, Truex had tried to lure him away from the world of interior design to be the design director at Tiffany's, and now that O'Brien was gone, he had every intention of again approaching Hadley about the job. He well remembered that fateful day in 1962 when Hadley had called him to say that while he remained on the best of terms with Mrs. Brown, he had resigned from his position at McMillen, Inc. When Truex heard the news,

Truex's last apartment in New York City. Collection of African and Oriental artifacts, detail.

he had become seriously worried about Hadley's future: walking away from a job at McMillen was not something to do on a whim. Fortunately, on the same day Hadley called him, Truex was scheduled to dine with his friend Mrs. Henry Parish II. In the course of the evening, Mrs. Parish confided to Truex that she was considering retiring; she said that she could not continue her decorating unless she found someone to take on some of the major responsibilities of her business. He immediately asked if she would be willing to consider Hadley. He explained that even though Hadley had resigned from McMillen, Inc., he and Mrs. Brown had parted company on good terms and remained friends. Mrs. Parish told Truex to have Hadley come around to her apartment the following afternoon. The meeting between Hadley and Mrs. Parish was serendipitous: they became partners in Parish-Hadley, Inc., soon to be one of the most respected interior design firms in the world. Hadley's success was one of Truex's great joys, and he was happy to know that he had played some small role in helping him to achieve it.

Besides Hadley, the Pierreponts were the only close friends Truex had left in New York City. After the sale of the Ménerbes house, John Pierrepont advised him on investing the money and arranged an appointment for him with Winthrop Rutherford, Jr., a lawyer at White and Case who would help him write his will and put his legal affairs in order. When Truex had first leased the apartment on East Sixty-third Street, in 1972, he had furnished it as simply as possible. He always said it was "like living in a box," but for now, it completely suited his purposes. His pair of Fazini sculptures, *The Diving Boys;* some small African primitive pieces; a few Chinese figures, including a small jade dog and a pair of bronze turtles supporting cranes; and his one piece of religious art, a nineteenth-century Italian figure of Christ carved out of wood, were the only decorative objects in the apartment. Odom's pair of Vieux Paris porcelain lamps; a wash drawing that Walter Gay had done and given to him; a pair of Louis-Phillippe papier-mâché chairs he had bought for

his first apartment in Paris; and his paintings by
Carlyle Brown were his few concessions to sentiment. Most of the paintings on the walls were his
own. He had given the majority of his work to the
Musée Calvet in Avignon before leaving Provence.

From his first days in New York as a student
in 1923, and certainly since his return from Paris
in 1939, Truex had been at the center of the city's
social and cultural excitement. As design director
for Tiffany's from 1955 until 1962, he had led a
charmed existence. But by 1978, he had been away
for almost sixteen years. In an interview, he told a
New York Times reporter, "I have rather dreaded returning to New York. I believe if you are in this
city you should be in the arena. This is not a place
for non-activists." His apprehensions were well
founded. When he went for his interview with the
admissions committee at the Knickerbocker Club,
the meeting was not a success, and it became the

Truex's last apartment in New York City. Dining table set with Wedgwood "Classic White" china, Tiffany "Bamboo" flatware, and "All-Purpose" wineglasses.

sad chore of one of his proposers to tell him that he had not been admitted.
The bearer of the news would later recall his attempt to ease the blow: "I told
him, 'Van, you've been out of New York for a long time, and several of the
members felt they didn't know you.' All of which was true." The embarrass-
ment of not being accepted as a member at the Knick confirmed Truex's decision to leave New York City.

Soon after he moved back to the States, Truex was tempted to buy a
Douglas Abdel sculpture, *Naexa-Alkyad,* from Andrew Crispo, but thinking it
too expensive, he hesitated for some months. Throughout the fall, he was
haunted by the sculpture and repeatedly stopped in at Crispo's gallery on East

Truex's last apartment in New York City. Living room.

Fifty-seventh Street just to admire it. Soon after the first of March, now confident that he would be moving to the country, he finally bought *Naexa-Alkyad*
as a birthday present for himself.

On the first weekend of March, Truex's friends put together several
small parties to celebrate his seventy-fifth birthday. Baldwin came from Nantucket to join him for the fetes. His English friends, Rory Cameron and the
Laurance Robertses, all called to wish him a happy birthday and good luck in
his search for a new house. Each of them, being a close friend, asked after his
health. He was careful to assure everyone that he was fine. All the while, he
knew that each day he was growing weaker. He continued to believe, however, that once he was out of the city and relieved of his responsibilities at
Tiffany's, he would begin to regain his strength.

After his weekend in Connecticut, Truex returned to New York on

Sunday evening feeling that he had found the perfect house in Litchfield County. In Saturday's mail, he found a letter from Walter Lees containing a touching reminiscence of the generous gift from Mona Bismarck that had allowed Lees to buy his apartment in London. Lees always referred to his London flat as "Mona's Place." On Monday morning, Truex felt more tired than usual and decided to stay in bed. He wasn't expecting any visitors, and his cleaning woman wasn't due until Wednesday. Since everyone thought he would be away until late Monday afternoon, he was completely alone all day and received no calls. That evening, after his customary supper—a cup of bouillon and a small serving of applesauce—he arranged his breakfast tray for the next morning. This nightly ritual was one of the first things Odom had taught him. He covered the tray with a freshly ironed white place mat and a matching linen napkin and then added his "Drabware" plate, cup, and saucer,

Truex's last apartment in New York City. Living room.

Truex's last apartment in New York City. Dining area.

a Tiffany silver "Bamboo" spoon, and a matching spreader for his confiture. One of Odom's many dictums was that it was better for one's figure to have toast without butter and leave croissants for people with bulging middles. On Tuesday, as usual, Truex was up at five-thirty in the morning. As was his custom when having breakfast alone, he put on his dressing gown, made himself some coffee, and settled in to read the morning paper.

John Pierrepont called Truex's apartment just after nine o'clock on Tuesday morning to find out how the weekend had gone and to get a report on the house search. Getting no answer, he phoned Tiffany's soon after ten and was told that Truex had not come in. When the day passed with no word from him, both Pierrepont and Hoving assumed that he had found his dream house in Connecticut and stayed over to begin the necessary real estate negotiations. Still, even if that was the case, it was unlike him not to call and tell them his plans had changed. But there was nothing Pierrepont or Hoving could do, since neither of them knew where Truex was staying in the country.

Pierrepont tried calling his friend's apartment that evening; when he got no answer, he decided that Truex probably was out for dinner somewhere. On Wednesday morning, just after nine o'clock, he called again. This time, the maid answered the telephone. She was hysterical. In her overwrought condition, she was barely able to explain that she had just come in and found Truex slumped over the breakfast table, dead. Beside him on the floor was the *New York Times* from the previous morning—Tuesday, April 24, 1979.

Walter Hoving's notice to the employees of Tiffany's, issued on April 25, said, "It grieves me to report to you that my good friend and your associate, Van Truex, died yesterday. His contribution to this company for the last many years cannot possibly be exaggerated." His words reflected the charmed partnership he had had with Truex, and the unwavering loyalty they had always shown each other. Throughout Truex's tenure at Tiffany's, his relationship with the company had been based on his personal arrangement with Walter Hoving; in all his twenty-four years there, he had never had a written contract.

Truex's aunt Kee was now in her nineties. Burdened with dementia since the early 1960s, she was confined to a nursing home. Her condition was

Truex's last apartment in New York City. Collection of African and Oriental artifacts.

such that she would never know about her nephew's death or, for that matter, the deaths of his siblings Phyllis and Herbert. This "determined, strong-willed woman," as she had once been described by a relative, had outlived the entire Truex family. Throughout his life, Truex had confided to his friends, "When my aunt Kee dies, my ship will come in. I know that I will be the chief beneficiary of her will, which will make me a very rich man." He was spared the knowledge that this was not the case. In her will, drawn up before her illness, she said she felt she had provided sufficiently for Truex when he needed money for his education. She designated a small bequest for him and specified larger amounts of money for Phyllis and Herbert, who had never fared well.

Truex had left specific instructions that after he died, his remains were to be cremated, and there was to be no funeral. Because his death was so sudden and, for most of his friends, so totally unexpected, John Pierrepont, the executor of his estate, felt there should be a memorial service. He arranged for the Reverend Hays Rockwell, the rector of Saint James's Episcopal Church, to conduct the service on Friday, May 4. Luminaries from the world of interior design and Tiffany's employees filled Saint James's to capacity. Sergio Pizzoni came from Washington, and Billy Baldwin from Nantucket. Immediately following the service, there was a reception, also arranged by John Pierrepont. It was held at the Knickerbocker Club.

When Rory Cameron heard the news, his greatest concern was for where Truex would be buried. When he was told that his friend's ashes were to be interred in Greenwood Cemetery in Brooklyn, Cameron asked that they instead be sent to France for interment in his garden in Ménerbes. Pierrepont saw no reason to not honor the request. In June, with only Cameron and his companion, Gilbert Occelli, present, Truex's ashes were buried at Les Quatre Sources. After the interment, Cameron created a formal French garden, approximately thirty by fifty feet, around the burial place. Amid plantings of low boxwood and tightly trimmed cotoneaster, the intersection of a vertical and a horizontal walkway, laid out in native limestone chipping stone, forms a Latin cross. At the axis of the cross stands a nine-foot-high limestone obelisk designed by Cameron. The inscription, cut into the base of the obelisk in a classic Roman font, reads simply "Van Day Truex." When Cameron died, six years later, in 1985, his ashes were scattered in the garden he had created for Truex. The present owner of Les Quatre Sources, Nicolas Krul, a Swiss investment banker, maintains the site as a revered part of the property.

The primary beneficiary of Truex's estate was the Metropolitan Museum of Art. In his will, he specified that he would like the income from his bequest to be used for the purchase of eighteenth-century French and Italian drawings, though he added that his directive was not binding upon the trustees. Since 1979, with the income from the Van Day Truex Fund, forty-six drawings have been added to the museum's permanent collection.

In November 1979, Ashton Hawkins arranged for a number of Truex's paintings and designs for Tiffany's and Baccarat to be shown in a special exhibit at the Metropolitan. From Truex's earliest days in New York, the museum had been an important part of his life. During his first year at the New York School of Fine and Applied Arts, in 1924, he had had his photograph taken on the massive front steps with three of his classmates. In 1980, his name was added to the list of the museum's most distinguished benefactors, carved into the stone wall of the staircase of the great entrance hall. This prestigious commemoration seems completely appropriate, but like all memorials, it falls short of capturing the spirit of the person being remembered. Truex's real memorial, his true legacy, consists in the countless designers and decorators whom he trained and influenced. Today these men and women, and those others who have in turn been influenced by them, still follow Van Day Truex's lead and continue his quest for the two most elusive qualities of art: beauty and simplicity.

Obelisk marking Truex's burial place, Les Quatre
Sources, the last home of Rory Cameron, near
Ménerbes, Provence.

Bibliography

Amory, Cleveland, and Frederic Bradlee, eds. *Vanity Fair: A Cavalcade of the 1920s and 1930s.* New York: Viking, 1960.

Astor, Brooke. *Footprints.* Garden City, N.J.: Doubleday, 1980.

Auchincloss, Louis. *Edith Wharton: A Woman in Her Time.* New York: Viking, 1971.

Aylesworth, Thomas G., and Virginia Aylesworth. *New York: The Glamour Years, 1919–1945.* New York: Gallery, 1987.

Baldwin, William W. *Billy Baldwin Decorates.* New York: Holt, Rinehart and Winston, 1973.

———. *Billy Baldwin Remembers.* New York: Harcourt Brace Jovanovich, 1974.

———, and Michael Gardine. *Billy Baldwin: An Autobiography.* Boston: Little, Brown, 1985.

Ballard, Bettina. *In My Fashion.* New York: David McKay, 1960.

Battersby, Martin. *The Decorative Thirties.* Rev. Philippe Garner. New York: Whitney Library of Design, 1988.

———. *The Decorative Twenties.* Rev. Philippe Garner. New York: Whitney Library of Design, 1988.

———. *Trompe l'Oeil: The Eye Deceived.* New York: St. Martin's, 1974.

———. *The World of Art Nouveau.* New York: Funk & Wagnall's, 1968.

Beaton, Cecil. *The Best of Beaton.* New York: Macmillan, 1968.

———. *Cecil Beaton's Scrapbook.* New York: Scribner's, 1937.

———. *The Face of the World: An International Scrapbook of People and Places.* New York: John Day, 1960.

———. *The Glass of Fashion.* Garden City, N.Y.: Doubleday, 1954.

———. *Memoirs of the Forties.* London: Weidenfeld and Nicolson, 1972.

———, and Kenneth Tynan. *Persona Grata.* New York: Putnam's, 1954.

Becker, Robert. *Nancy Lancaster: Her Life, Her World, Her Art.* New York: Knopf, 1996.

Bemelmans, Ludwig. *To the One I Love the Best: Episodes from the Life of Lady Mendl.* New York: Viking, 1955.

Bernier, Georges, and Rosamond Bernier, eds. *European Decoration: Creative Contemporary Interiors.* New York: Morrow, 1969.

Bernier, Olivier. *Fireworks at Dusk: Paris in the Thirties.* Boston: Little, Brown, 1993.

Bloch, Michael. *The Duchess of Windsor.* New York: St. Martin's, 1996.

Brown, Erica. *Sixty Years of Interior Design: The World of McMillen.* New York: Viking, 1982.

Brunhammer, Yvonne, and Suzanne Tise. *The Decorative Arts in France, 1900–1942.* New York: Rizzoli, 1990.

Camard, Florence. *Ruhlmann: Master of Art Deco.* New York: Thames and Hudson, 1984.

Cameron, Roderick. *The Golden Riviera.* London: Weidenfeld and Nicolson, 1975.

Campbell, Nina, and Caroline Seebohm. *Elsie de Wolfe: A Decorative Life.* New York: Clarkson N. Potter, 1992.

Castle, Charles. *Oliver Messel.* London: Thames and Hudson, 1986.

Chanaux, Adolfe. *Jean-Michel Frank.* Paris: Editions du Regard, 1997.

Charles-Roux, Edmonde. *Chanel and Her World.* New York: Vendome, 1981.

Chawncey, George. *Gay New York.* New York: HarperCollins, 1994.

Cipriani, Arrigo. *Harry's Bar: The Life and Times of the Legendary Venice Landmark.* New York: Arcade, 1996.

Coleman, Elizabeth A. *The Genius of Charles James.* New York: Holt, Rinehart and Winston, 1982.

Core, Philip. *The Original Eye: Arbiters of Twentieth-Century Taste.* London: Quartet, 1984.

Cornin, Vincent. *Paris, City of Light, 1919–1939.* London: HarperCollins, 1994.

Cowles, Fleur, ed. *The Best of* Flair. New York: HarperCollins, 1996.

Curry, Mary Elizabeth. *Creating an American Institution: The Merchandising Genius of J. C. Penney.* New York: Garland, 1993.

Curtis, Charlotte. *The Rich and Other Atrocities.* New York: Harper & Row, 1976.

de Wolfe, Elsie. *The House in Good Taste.* New York: Century, 1914.

Donovan, Carrie. *Living Well: The* New York Times *Book of Home Design and Decoration.* New York: Times Books, 1981.

Douglas, Murray, and Chippy Irvine. *Brunschwig & Fils Style.* Boston: Bulfinch, 1995.

Drake, Nicholas. *The Fifties in* Vogue. New York: Holt, 1987.

Dwight, Eleanor. *Edith Wharton: An Extraordinary Life.* New York: Abrams, 1994.

Esten, John, and Rose Bennett Gilbert. *Manhattan Style.* Boston: Little, Brown, 1990.

Faucigny-Lucinge, Jean-Louis de. *Legendary Parties, 1922–1972.* New York: Vendome, 1987.

Fisher, Richard B. *Syrie Maugham.* London: Duckworth, 1978.

Flanner, Janet. *London Was Yesterday, 1934–1939.* New York: Viking, 1975.

———. *Paris Was Yesterday, 1925–1939.* New York: Viking, 1972.

Foucart, Bruno, and Jean-Louis Gaillemin. *Les Décorateurs des années 40.* Paris: Norma Editions, 1998.

———, et al. Normandie: *Queen of the Seas.* New York: Vendome, 1985.

Friedman, Barry. *Bernard Boutet de Monvel.* New York: Barry Friedman, 1994.

Hall, Carolyn. *The Forties in* Vogue. New York: Harmony, 1985.

———. *The Thirties in* Vogue. New York: Harmony, 1985.

———. *The Twenties in* Vogue. New York: Harmony, 1983.

Hampton, Mark. *Legendary Decorators of the Twentieth Century.* New York: Doubleday, 1992.

———. *Mark Hampton on Decorating.* New York: Random House, 1989.

Hoare, Philip. *Noël Coward*. New York: Simon and Schuster, 1995.

Holme, Bryan, et al., eds. *The World in* Vogue. New York: Viking, 1963.

Kaiser, Charles. *The Gay Metropolis, 1940–1996*. Boston: Houghton Mifflin, 1997.

Karnow, Stanley. *Paris in the Fifties*. New York: Random House, 1997.

Kazanjian, Dodie, and Calvin Tompkins. *Alex: The Life of Alexander Liberman*. New York: Knopf, 1993.

Klüver, Billy, and Julie Martin. *Kiki's Paris: Artists and Lovers, 1900–1930*. New York: Abrams, 1989.

Kochno, Boris. *Bérard*. London: Thames and Hudson, 1988.

———. *Diaghilev and the Ballets Russes*. New York: Harper & Row, 1970.

Lawford, Valentine. *Horst: His Work and His World*. New York: Knopf, 1984.

———. Vogue*'s Book of Houses, Gardens, People*. New York: Viking, 1968.

Lesley, Cole. *Remembered Laughter: The Life of Noël Coward*. New York: Knopf, 1976.

Lewis, Hilary, and John O'Connor. *Philip Johnson: The Architect in His Own Words*. New York: Rizzoli, 1994.

Loring, John. *Tiffany Taste*. New York: Doubleday, 1986.

———, and Henry B. Platt. *The New Tiffany Table Settings*. Garden City, N.Y.: Doubleday, 1981.

Lottman, Herbert. *Colette*. Boston: Little, Brown, 1991.

Loughery, John. *The Other Side of Silence: Men's Lives and Gay Identities: A Twentieth-Century History*. New York: Holt, 1998.

McBrien, William. *Cole Porter*. New York: Knopf, 1998.

Mann, Carol. *Paris between the Wars*. New York: Vendome, 1996.

Mann, William J. *Wisecracker: The Life and Times of William Haines, Hollywood's First Openly Gay Star*. New York: Viking, 1998.

Mellow, James R. *Charmed Circle: Gertrude Stein & Company*. New York: Praeger, 1974.

Menkes, Suzy. *The Windsor Style*. Topsfield, Mass.: Salem House, 1988.

Metcalf, Pauline C. *Ogden Codman and the Decoration of Houses*. Boston: Boston Atheneum and Godine, 1988.

Mohrt, Françoise. *The Givenchy Style.* New York: Vendome, 1998.

Moore, Gene. *Windows at Tiffany's.* New York: Abrams, 1980.

————, and Jay Hyams. *My Time at Tiffany's.* New York: St. Martin's, 1990.

Morris, Jan. *Manhattan '45.* New York: Oxford, 1987.

Pahlmann, William. *The Pahlmann Book of Interior Design.* New York: Crowell, 1955.

Parish, Sister, Albert Hadley, and Christopher Petkanas. *Parish-Hadley: Sixty Years of American Design.* New York: Little, Brown, 1995.

Parsons, Frank Alvah. *Interior Decoration: Its Principles and Practice.* New York: Doubleday, 1915.

Patterson, Jerry E. *Fifth Avenue: The Best Address.* New York: Rizzoli, 1998.

Plimpton, George. *Truman Capote.* New York: Doubleday, 1997.

Pochna, Marie-France. *Christian Dior: The Man Who Made the World Look New.* New York: Arcade, 1996.

Pohorilenko, Anatole, and James Crump. *When We Were Three: The Travel Albums of George Platt Lynes, Monroe Wheeler, and Glenway Westcott, 1925–1935.* San Francisco: Arena, 1998.

Pool, Mary Jane, ed. *Twentieth-Century Decorating, Architecture & Gardens: Eighty Years of Ideas and Pleasure from* House and Garden. New York: Holt, Rinehart and Winston, 1980.

Purtell, Joseph. *The Tiffany Touch.* New York: Random House, 1971.

Rasponi, Lanfranco. *The Golden Oasis.* New York: Putnam's, 1968.

————. *The International Nomads.* New York: Putnam's, 1966.

Robsjohn-Gibbings, T. H. *Good-bye, Mr. Chippendale.* New York: Knopf, 1944.

————. *Homes of the Brave.* New York: Knopf, 1954.

————, and Carlton W. Pullin. *Furniture of Classical Greece.* New York: Knopf, 1963.

Ross, Josephine. *Beaton in* Vogue. New York: Clarkson N. Potter, 1986.

————. *Society in* Vogue. New York: Vendome, 1992.

Russell, John. *Paris.* New York: Abrams, 1983.

Russell, Vivian. *Edith Wharton's Italian Gardens.* Boston: Bulfinch, 1997.

Seebohm, Caroline. *The Man Who Was* Vogue: *The Life and Times of Condé Nast.* New York: Viking, 1982.

Skurka, Norma. *The New York Times Book of Interior Design and Decoration.* New York: Quadrangle/The New York Times Book Co., Inc. 1976.

Smith, Jane S. *Elsie de Wolfe: A Life in the High Style.* New York: Atheneum, 1982.

Souhami, Diana. *Mrs. Keppel and Her Daughter.* New York: St. Martin's, 1997.

Spencer, Charles. *Leon Bakst and the Ballets Russes.* London: Academy, 1995.

Tapert, Annette, and Diana Edkins. *The Power of Style.* New York: Crown, 1994.

Tauranac, John, and Christopher Little. *Elegant New York: The Builders and the Buildings.* New York: Abbeville, 1985.

Tiffany & Co. *Tiffany Table Settings.* New York: Crowell, 1960.

Trahey, Jane, ed. Harper's Bazaar: *One Hundred Years of the American Female.* New York: Random House, 1967.

Truex, Van Day. *Interiors, Character and Color.* Los Angeles: Knapp, 1980.

Vaill, Amanda. *Everybody Was So Young: Gerald and Sara Murphy—A Lost Generation Love Story.* Boston: Houghton Mifflin, 1998.

Varney, Carleton. *The Draper Touch: The High Life and High Style of Dorothy Draper.* New York: Prentice-Hall, 1988.

Vickers, Hugo. *Cecil Beaton.* Boston: Little, Brown, 1985.

———. *The Private World of the Duke and Duchess of Windsor.* London: Harrods, 1995.

Vreeland, Diana. *Allure.* Garden City, N.Y.: Doubleday, 1980.

———. *D.V.* New York: Knopf, 1984.

Wallach, Janet. *Chanel: Her Style and Her Life.* New York: Doubleday, 1998.

Weber, Nicholas Fox. *Patron Saints: Five Rebels Who Opened America to a New Art, 1924–1943.* New Haven, Conn.: Yale, 1995.

Wharton, Edith, and Ogden Codman, Jr. *The Decoration of Houses.* Reprint, New York: Norton, 1978.

White, Palmer. *Elsa Schiaparelli.* New York: Rizzoli, 1986.

Wiser, William. *The Crazy Years: Paris in the Twenties.* London: Thames and Hudson, 1990.

Writings by Van Day Truex

"Mirrors of Personality: Lecture Given at the Decorators Club." *Interiors*, December 1940.

"The Environment for Creating Good Design." In *The Art of Design Management: Design in American Business*. Philadelphia: University of Pennsylvania Press, 1975.

"Jean-Michel Frank Remembered." *Architectural Digest*, September–October 1976.

"Van Day Truex on Design: A Journey to India." *Architectural Digest*, January 1977.

"Guest Speaker: The Nuances of Interior Lighting." *Architectural Digest*, March 1977.

"Van Day Truex on Design: An Unusual Museum at Avignon." *Architectural Digest*, May–June 1977.

"Van Day Truex on Design: The Public Look versus the Private Look." *Architectural Digest*, July–August 1977.

"Van Day Truex on Design: Responsibility in Design." *Architectural Digest*, September 1977.

"Van Day Truex on Design: Reproduction Furniture: The Pros and Cons." *Architectural Digest*, October 1977.

"Guest Speaker: Some Small Miracles." *Architectural Digest*, November 1977.

"Van Day Truex on Design: Private Rooms." *Architectural Digest*, April 1978.

"Van Day Truex on Design: Interiors, Character and Color." *Architectural Digest*, September 1978.

"Guest Speaker: The Magic of the Mirror." *Architectural Digest*, October 1978.

"Guest Speaker: The Pleasure of Scrapbooks." *Architectural Digest,* January–February 1979.

"La Commanderie: French Designer Restores an Ancient Stronghold." *Architectural Digest,* November 1979.

Index